FROM CONFLICT TO COMMUNION

REFORMATION RESOURCES, 1517–2017

SERIES EDITORS

Norman A. Hjelm, Philip D. Krey, and William G. Rusch

From Conflict to Communion

LUTHERAN-CATHOLIC COMMON COMMEMORATION
OF THE REFORMATION IN 2017

*The Lutheran World Federation
and the Pontifical Council for Promoting Christian Unity*

....

with an Introduction by
William G. Rusch
....

A Study Guide to From Conflict to Communion
....

Common Prayer for the Ecumenical Commemoration
Lund, Sweden, October 31, 2016
....

*Lutheran and Roman Catholic Vespers
with Propers for the Unity of the Church*

WILLIAM B. EERDMANS PUBLISHING COMPANY
GRAND RAPIDS, MICHIGAN

Wm. B. Eerdmans Publishing Co.
2140 Oak Industrial Drive NE
Grand Rapids, MI 49505
www.eerdmans.com

© 2017 Pontifical Council for Promoting Christian Unity, Lutheran World Federation, and
Wm. B. Eerdmans Publishing Co.
North American edition published 2017

Previously published portions of this book:
From Conflict to Communion © 2013 by Evangelische Verlagsanstalt GmbH, Leipzig,
Germany, and Bonifatius GmbH Paderborn, Germany
Study Guide: From Conflict to Communion © 2015 Roman Catholic Diocese of Pittsburgh
and Southwestern Pennsylvania Synod of the Evangelical Lutheran Church

Printed in the United States of America

23 22 21 20 19 18 17   1 2 3 4 5 6 7

ISBN 978-0-8028-7377-4

Library of Congress Cataloging-in-Publication Data

A catalog record for this book is available from the Library of Congress

Contents

Introduction to the American Edition

William G. Rusch

The purpose of this introduction is to provide for the general reader the background and the context of *From Conflict to Communion: Lutheran-Catholic Common Commemoration of the Reformation in 2017*, a report produced by the Lutheran–Roman Catholic Commission on Unity (the international Lutheran–Roman Catholic Dialogue). The commission is sponsored by the Lutheran World Federation and the Pontifical Council for Promoting Christian Unity of the Vatican. The footnotes that accompany this introduction offer resources to explore more deeply the history and motivations that resulted in this dialogue report, focused on the 500th anniversary of the Reformation.

Both the Scriptures and the creeds bear witness to the fact that the unity of the Church belongs to the Church's very being. The unity of Christ's Church is not a desired characteristic for convenience or efficiency, although unity may enhance those attributes. Rather, the unity of the Church is an essential dimension of the Church's nature. This insight has been described as "the basic ecumenical conviction." This essential unity of the Church has been regarded as a prerequisite or presupposition for every attempt on the part of churches to give expression to their unity. This perception has been expressed as "the ecumenical indicative." Both this conviction and this indicative have led many churches and individuals to "the ecumenical imperative," viz., that the essential unity of the Church must be lived and not be a mere abstraction; it must be visible. It is this imperative that supplies the motivation and aim of the modern ecumenical movement—to allow God's given unity to Christ's people, the Church, to be made visible.[1]

1. These concepts and their history can be explored further in Harding Meyer, *That All*

William G. Rusch is professor (adjunct) of Lutheran studies at the Divinity School of Yale University.

Yet it is well known that, in the history of the Church, its visible unity has not been obvious but absent. The story of the Church has been a sad narrative of divisions, polemics, caricatures, and even violence. This unfortunate state of affairs was especially transparent in the division between the western and eastern churches in the eleventh century and in the sixteenth-century Reformation events in the western church.

The modern ecumenical movement, whose origin at least in part is located in the World Missionary Conference at Edinburgh in 1910, arose to address precisely the issue of the scandal of the visible disunity of the Church, particularly on the mission fields. The history of the Church in the twentieth century can largely be spelled out in terms of the developments flowing from the Edinburgh Conference.

Two areas of ecumenical activity were quickly identified. They were the Life and Work movement, devoted to social and ethical issues that divided the churches, and the Faith and Order movement, which concentrated on the theological topics that prevented greater unity among the churches. In the 1920s and 1930s both of these movements sponsored international conferences to promote their work. These two enterprises joined together in 1948 to form the World Council of Churches. In 1961 the International Missionary Council, representing the concerns of the Edinburgh Conference, joined the World Council of Churches. Many similar councils of churches were established in various countries around the world.[2]

Initial Lutheran reactions to such developments ranged from hostile to cautious, based on concerns about the fear of doctrinal compromise in an equation of the Church's faith with its order. Gradually many of these Lutheran anxieties subsided, and many Lutherans and their churches globally and in numerous nations joined in the ecumenical effort. Lutherans had begun to read their confessional documents (*The Book of Concord*) in such a manner that they saw themselves, because of their confessions, committed

---

May Be One (Grand Rapids: Eerdmans, 1999), 1–15. To give two examples, it is these concepts and commitments that underlie the Roman Catholic Church's Decree on Ecumenism of the Second Vatican Council. See Norman Tanner, SJ, ed., *Decrees of the Ecumenical Councils*, vol. 2 (London: Sheed & Ward; Washington, DC: Georgetown University Press, 1990), 908–20, and the Evangelical Lutheran Church in America's statement, *Ecumenism: The Commitment of the Evangelical Lutheran Church in America* (Minneapolis: Augsburg Fortress, 1994).

2. For an overview of this history, see William G. Rusch, *A Movement toward Church Unity: Ecumenism* (Philadelphia: Fortress, 1985), 19–33, and John Briggs, Mercy Amba Oduyoye, and George Tsetsis, eds., *A History of the Ecumenical Movement*, vol. 3 (Geneva: World Council of Churches, 2004).

to the oneness of Christ's Church.[3] This was quite a departure from some earlier Lutheran thinking.

During the early decades of ecumenical history, the Roman Catholic Church officially stood apart from these efforts of Life and Work and Faith and Order. It declined to pursue membership in the World Council of Churches. The official position of the Roman Catholic Church was that Christian unity could be restored only by the return of non-Catholic individuals and churches to the Roman Catholic Church. This is the stance set forth in Pope Pius XI's encyclical, *Mortalium Animos* of 1928. This point of view shifted only slightly in 1950 with the instruction of the Holy See, *Ecclesia Catholica*, which, while warning of the dangers of the ecumenical movement, did recognize the activity of the Holy Spirit in the movement.

This situation was altered dramatically by the Second Vatican Council (1962–65) and especially its two documents, the Constitution on the Church (*Lumen Gentium*) and the Decree on Ecumenism (*Unitatis Reintegratio*), both promulgated in November of 1964.[4] These two documents were an indication of the fact that the Roman Catholic Church had officially adopted a new ecclesiology. By acknowledging that the Church of Christ *subsists* in the Roman Catholic Church, and not that the Roman Catholic Church *is* the Church of Jesus Christ, the Council provided a way for the Roman Catholic Church, even though it has not entered the World Council of Churches, to participate in the one ecumenical movement. "Return to Rome" was no longer the dominant plea from the Vatican.

One of the most significant outcomes of the Second Vatican Council and the entry of the Roman Catholic Church into the one ecumenical movement was a new emphasis on bilateral, official, theological dialogue between divided churches. There is evidence of such dialogues earlier in the ecumenical movement, but a new chapter in this activity began as a result of the Second Vatican Council. From the Roman Catholic perspective, such dialogues allowed the Catholic Church to relate directly on a one-to-one basis with other churches, offering forums to explore, and perhaps even resolve, the theological issues that separated two churches or traditions.

The clear preference of the Roman Catholic Church in its ecumenical work was not the earlier Faith and Order model of organic union, but rather relationships of *full communion* with individual churches based on

3. Robert Kolb and Timothy J. Wengert, eds., *The Book of Concord: The Confessions of the Evangelical Lutheran Church* (Minneapolis: Fortress, 2000).
4. Tanner, ed., *Decrees of the Ecumenical Councils*, 2:845–900 and 908–20.

theological consensus and the overcoming of divisive judgments of the past. It is no accident that there was a virtual explosion of such dialogues after the Council. Not all these dialogues involved the Roman Catholic Church, although a considerable number did.

A number of churches and ecclesial traditions welcomed the opportunity for official theological conversations with the Roman Catholic Church on international and national levels. Lutherans were included in that group. Even before the Second Vatican Council had concluded at least one Lutheran observer at the Council suggested an international Lutheran–Roman Catholic dialogue.

Soon, planning for international and United States Lutheran–Roman Catholic dialogues occurred. Based on earlier work, a "Joint Working Group" between the Lutheran World Federation and the Secretariat for Promoting Christian Unity of the Vatican proposed an international Roman Catholic–Lutheran dialogue. The dialogue began its work in 1967 and issued the "Malta Report" on *The Gospel and the Church* in 1972.[5] The clarity, breadth, and boldness of this first report from the dialogue are evident, for it covered a wide range of topics. This first product of the Roman Catholic–Lutheran Commission on Unity was followed in following years by other texts: *The Eucharist* in 1978 claimed an agreement on eucharistic presence and sacrifice.[6] *Ways to Community* in 1980 provided a description of the goal of the dialogue.[7] *Ministry in the Church* in 1981 took up the topic of mutual Lutheran and Roman Catholic recognition of ministries.[8] *Facing Unity* in 1984 outlined a possible process by which, over a period of time, there could be a formation of a joint Lutheran-Catholic ministry.[9]

In 1980, the 450th anniversary of the Augsburg Confession, the dialogue published a statement, *All under One Christ*, which noted the ecumenical potential of this Lutheran confessional document.[10] In 1983, the 500th anniversary of Luther's birth, the dialogue released *Martin Luther—Witness*

5. See Harding Meyer and Lukas Vischer, eds., *Growth in Agreement: Reports and Agreed Statements of Ecumenical Conversations on a World Level* (New York/Ramsey: Paulist Press; Geneva: World Council of Churches, 1984), 168–89.

6. Meyer and Vischer, eds., *Growth in Agreement*, 190–214.

7. Meyer and Vischer, eds., *Growth in Agreement*, 215–40.

8. Meyer and Vischer, eds., *Growth in Agreement*, 248–75.

9. See Jeffrey Gros, FSC, Harding Meyer, and William G. Rusch, eds., *Growth in Agreement II: Reports and Agreed Statements of Ecumenical Conversations on a World Level, 1982–1998* (Geneva: World Council of Churches; Grand Rapids: Eerdmans, 2000), 443–84.

10. Meyer and Vischer, eds., *Growth in Agreement*, 241–47.

to Jesus Christ.[11] The text presented a portrait of Luther largely indebted to Roman Catholic scholarship of the twentieth century that moved beyond past polemics.

In 1994 the dialogue report *The Church and Justification* was released.[12] This dialogue report explored the ecclesiological implications of the doctrine of justification. In 2006 *The Apostolicity of the Church*, a study document from the dialogue, addressed this subject by means of a historical review.[13] The document acknowledges the importance of the *Joint Declaration on the Doctrine of Justification* of 1999 for its work.

On October 31, 1999, in Augsburg, Germany, representatives of the Lutheran World Federation and the Vatican signed the *Joint Declaration on the Doctrine of Justification.*[14] This text was based on the work of the Lutheran–Roman Catholic dialogue over the years. It demonstrated that the subscribing Lutheran churches and the Roman Catholic Church are able to express a common, though not total, understanding of justification by God's grace through faith in Christ. The result of such a common understanding is that the mutual condemnations of the sixteenth century between these churches on this topic no longer apply to the churches in question. The Joint Declaration with its concept of differentiated consensus is to be seen as the initial, and to date only, step in the official reception of this dialogue's work by the churches.[15]

This history of the international dialogue or commission has close parallels with developments in the United States. In 1965, after two years of preliminary conversations, the USA National Committee of the Lutheran World Federation and the Roman Catholic Bishops' Commission for Ecumenical Affairs approved a formal dialogue. This bilateral conversation has involved churches representing most of the Lutherans in the United States. The strategy from the outset was to begin with easier topics and move to more difficult items.

---

11. Gros, Meyer, and Rusch, eds., *Growth in Agreement II*, 438–42.

12. Gros, Meyer, and Rusch, eds., *Growth in Agreement II*, 485–565.

13. *Apostolicity of the Church: Study Document of the Lutheran–Roman Catholic Commission on Unity* (Minneapolis: Lutheran University Press, 2006).

14. Gros, Meyer, and Rusch, eds., *Growth in Agreement II*, 566–82. Also, the Lutheran World Federation and the Roman Catholic Church, *Joint Declaration on the Doctrine of Justification* (Grand Rapids: Eerdmans, 2000).

15. On the concept of "differentiated consensus," see William G. Rusch, *Ecumenical Reception: Its Challenge and Opportunity* (Grand Rapids: Eerdmans, 2007), 118–30, and also Harding Meyer, "'Einheit in versöhnter Verschiedenheit.' Eine ökumenische Zielvorstellung, Ihre Absicht, Entstehung und Bedeutung," *Kerygma und Dogma* 61, no. 2 (2015): 83–106, and esp. 97–99.

The document *The Status of the Nicene Creed as Dogma of the Church* appeared in 1965. This text was followed in 1966 by *One Baptism for the Remission of Sins. The Eucharist as Sacrifice* was released in 1967. Titles are descriptive of the contents of the reports. As the topics increased in difficulty, the time period between dialogue reports increased.

Thus in 1970 the dialogue published *Eucharist and Ministry*.[16] Four years later, *Papal Primacy and the Universal Church* was issued.[17] The level of agreement on this topic, so divisive in history, astonished many Catholics and Lutherans. An even more intractable problem in Lutheran–Roman Catholic relations, papal infallibility, was discussed between 1973 and 1978. In 1980 the dialogue report *Teaching Authority and Infallibility in the Church*, a volume of 336 pages, appeared.[18]

From 1979 until 1983 the dialogue took up a topic that had been touched upon or alluded to in earlier dialogue work: justification by faith. In 1985 the dialogue report, *Justification by Faith*, appeared, identifying a number of items of convergence and consensus.[19] This report contributed significantly to the *Joint Declaration on the Doctrine of Justification* described earlier. *The One Mediator, the Saints, and Mary*, which addressed the subject of sanctification and the saints, was released in 1992.[20] This was followed in 1995 with a slim report bearing the title *Scripture and Tradition*.[21] In 2005 the dialogue released and published its tenth report, *The Church as Koinonia of Salvation: Its Structures and Ministries*.[22] In 2011

16. The first three dialogue reports were published as Paul C. Empie and T. Austin Murphy, eds., *Lutherans and Catholics in Dialogue I–III* (Minneapolis: Augsburg, n.d.). *Eucharist and Ministry* was published as *Lutherans and Catholics in Dialogue IV* (New York: USA National Committee of the Lutheran World Federation; Washington, DC: Bishops' Committee for Ecumenical and Interreligious Affairs, 1970).

17. Paul C. Empie and T. Austin Murphy, eds., *Papal Primacy and the Universal Church: Lutherans and Catholic in Dialogue V* (Minneapolis: Augsburg, 1974).

18. Paul C. Empie, T. Austin Murphy, and Joseph A. Burgess, eds., *Teaching Authority and Infallibility in the Church: Lutherans and Catholics in Dialogue VI* (Minneapolis: Augsburg, 1978).

19. H. George Anderson, T. Austin Murphy, and Joseph A. Burgess, eds., *Justification by Faith: Lutherans and Catholics in Dialogue VII* (Minneapolis: Augsburg, 1985).

20. H. George Anderson, J. Francis Stafford, and Joseph A. Burgess, eds., *The One Mediator, the Saints, and Mary: Lutherans and Catholics in Dialogue VIII* (Minneapolis: Augsburg, 1992).

21. Harold C. Skillrud, J. Francis Stafford, and Daniel F. Martensen, eds., *Scripture and Tradition: Lutherans and Catholics in Dialogue IX* (Minneapolis: Augsburg, 1995).

22. Randall Lee and Jeffrey Gros, FSC, eds., *The Church as Koinonia of Salvation: Its Structures and Ministries: Lutherans and Catholics in Dialogue X* (Washington, DC: United States Conference of Catholic Bishops, 2005).

the most recent results of the dialogue, entitled *The Hope of Eternal Life*, were issued.[23]

In 2015 both the international and United States dialogues celebrated fifty years of continuous and serious theological scholarship by Catholics and Lutherans together. The purpose of this enterprise has been to confront the *theological* issues that caused division in the sixteenth century and that have kept Catholics and Lutherans in visible disunity since that time.

A careful study of the thousands of pages of reports from these dialogues, and other national dialogues, reveals an amazing number of convergences and consensus on subjects that until even recently were deemed both intractable and church-dividing. Certainly no one could responsibly claim that these dialogues have resolved all the issues that distinguish Catholics and Lutherans from each other, let alone all the items that seem sufficiently weighty to cause the division of churches. Nevertheless, the final and objective evaluation by many churches, individual theologians, and church leaders has been that these dialogues must be given the highest approbation. Their sponsoring churches owe profound gratitude to the women and men who participated in these countless meetings and drafting sessions.

The year 2015, however, marked not only a time of celebration for fifty years of ecumenical collaboration after centuries of isolation and polemic. It also began a period of ever more intense reflection about the upcoming year of 2017, the 500th anniversary of the Lutheran Reformation. Martin Luther had in 1517 issued his "Ninety-five Theses." This event, whether or not it involved a posting on a castle church door, has been viewed as a convenient marker for the start of the sixteenth-century events that have come to be portrayed as "the Reformation."

Since the sixteenth century, four centennial anniversaries have occurred. As would be expected, cultural, political, and religious factors influenced each of these occasions. The 100th anniversary in 1617 took place in a time of Roman Catholic retrenchment after the Council of Trent (1545–63) and a period of developing Lutheran Orthodoxy with its stress on dogmatic rigor and Lutheran distinctiveness over against both Catholicism and Calvinism. Two hundred years after the Reformation, Pietism had become a force in Europe. By 1817 both Catholic and Lutheran churches had confronted the Enlightenment, begun in the previous century, and a Europe in upheaval. In 1917 the world was experiencing an armed conflict without

---

23. Lowell G. Almen and Richard J. Sklba, eds., *The Hope of Eternal Life: Lutherans and Catholics in Dialogue XI* (Minneapolis: Lutheran University Press, 2011).

parallel to that time. In this setting, Luther was claimed by some nations and individuals as a national hero. A "new world order" was coming into existence. Confidence in human capacity for a better world was shattered.

With all these differences, common characteristics marked these four anniversaries. All of them were marked by an isolation of the two parties, often including contention between Lutherans and Roman Catholics. They had been living apart from each other for centuries. Their identities were shaped by their differences, and not by the common Christian message and heritage that they did have.

It is these factors that make the 500th anniversary of the Reformation unique. This commemoration in 2017 will not be marked by isolation or conflict. It will be based on a fifty-year period of profound theological dialogue and a growing relation of closer ties, indicated by visits, faculty exchanges, and joint parish study groups. Thus a new challenge happily arises: in an ecumenical age, how should Catholics and Lutherans note the Reformation? This challenge obviously has implications for other Reformation churches as well.

Already in advance of the fiftieth anniversary of the dialogues and the 500th commemoration of the Lutheran Reformation, attention began to be focused on how to mark the anniversary of this Reformation in an ecumenical age. In 2009 the international dialogue started to reflect on the possibilities. In 2013 the international Lutheran–Roman Catholic Commission on Unity (the international Lutheran–Roman Catholic dialogue) published in English, Finnish, German, Polish, and Spanish the text entitled in English *From Conflict to Communion*.[24] These circumstances gave the document an unusual if not unique character in comparison with other reports published previously by the commission. This is true even of the reports marking the anniversaries of the Augsburg Confession and of Martin Luther.

From Conflict to Communion has as its purpose to prepare Lutherans and Roman Catholics for an upcoming event, viz. 2017. Even the manner of describing the anniversary presents its challenges. Some Lutherans may believe that the event should be only a "celebration." They wish to hold up the contributions and benefits of the Reformation to the Church and the world. Other Lutherans, and certainly most Catholics, have difficulty in combining the notion of "celebration" with an event, whatever its positive features, that caused division in the western church and much hardship for Lutherans,

24. See https://www.lutheranworld.org/content/resource-conflict-communion -basis-lutheran-catholic-commemoration-reformation-2017.

Roman Catholics, and others. The English text addresses this problem by the use of the word "commemoration."

From Conflict to Communion wishes to present the occasion of 2017 as an opportunity for deeper communion between Lutherans and Roman Catholics and for the celebration of the common witness they share to the gospel of Jesus Christ. It does this by an integration of fundamental themes of Luther's theology and the contemporary Catholic response to this theology. It stresses that on these issues Lutherans and Catholics can now speak with one voice if not total agreement. To be adequately appreciated, *From Conflict to Communion* should be read in the light of the dialogue reports, and especially the *Joint Declaration on the Doctrine of Justification.*

Although *From Conflict to Communion* gives considerable attention to past history and recognizes continuing differences between Lutherans and Catholics, it points to the consensus already achieved. Thus it seeks to be a resource not only for Catholic and Lutheran church leaders and theologians but also for Lutheran and Roman Catholic people around the world.[25]

Its desired audience and the nature of its task present a number of potential problems. There is a need to explain a good deal of history that may not be common knowledge to many persons. There is the story of ecumenical developments and of the specific vocabulary that ecumenism has developed over its years of work. These factors have led early to the conclusion that *From Conflict to Communion* would be well served to have an accompanying study guide, which this edition includes, and suitable liturgical material that could be utilized in appropriate joint Catholic-Lutheran worship.

By the nature of its designed purpose and the fact that *From Conflict to Communion* originates in a dialogue group or commission, there is one thing that this text cannot do: it cannot be the vehicle by which the results of fifty years of dialogue on international and national levels are *officially* and *juridically* received by the churches. For this task, a different type of ecumenical document and process is required. Nevertheless, *From Conflict to Communion* can contribute much to an atmosphere of trust and comfort

---

25. In March of 2014, the Reverend Martin Junge, the general secretary of the Lutheran World Federation, and Cardinal Kurt Koch, the president of the Pontifical Council for Promoting Christian Unity, together issued a letter encouraging joint study between Lutherans and Catholics of *From Conflict to Communion* at levels appropriate to their respective contexts and ecumenical realities. Unpublished letter of March 18, 2014, from the Lutheran World Federation, Geneva, and the Pontifical Council for Promoting Christian Unity, the Vatican. See also *Istina* 58, no. 3 (2013), an issue devoted to *From Conflict to Communion, Du conflit à la communion,* with articles by M. Efdou, M. Lienhard, and U. Körtner.

between formerly estranged Catholics and Lutherans that would make future ecumenical reception a reality.[26]

In view of the purpose of *From Conflict to Communion*, certain characteristics of the document should be expected. First, it is largely instructive and informational. It wishes to share a narrative of a history and recent interpretations of that history. Its goal is to engage a general readership rather than an academic community. Yet at the same time it must convey a certain amount of rather technical information. These two characteristics present challenges that are not present in many other dialogue reports.

Second, its stated goal relates specifically to *Lutheran* and *Roman Catholic* events leading up to and in the year 2017. Therefore *From Conflict to Communion* does not address certain topics, such as other Reformation churches and their relation at the present time to the Roman Catholic Church, and Luther's complex and unfortunate relations to the Jews of his day.[27] In a scholarly treatise more could be expected about Luther's connection to the teachings of William Ockham. On the other hand, and in light of the intention of the work, the reader could have anticipated more attention to the papacy, the Second Vatican Council, ethical issues that are potentially church dividing, and even indulgences in view of their sixteenth-century importance. The papacy, the Second Vatican Council, and indulgences are topics of only one or two paragraphs each.

The entire text of *From Conflict to Communion* is 87 pages. After a foreword and an introduction, it contains six chapters and an appendix. Again, it can be assumed that its pedagogical aim influenced its length.

After the foreword and introduction, both of which highlight the year 2017, chapter one takes up the topic of commemorating the Reformation in an ecumenical and global age. It points to the uniqueness of this situation and the challenges it presents for both Lutherans and Catholics.

Chapter two presents new perspectives that have come forth in the

---

26. For a discussion of "ecumenical reception," see Rusch, *Ecumenical Reception: Its Challenge and Opportunity.* The only example of such Lutheran–Roman Catholic reception to date is the *Joint Declaration on the Doctrine of Justification.* For an account of this process, see William G. Rusch, "The History and Methodology of the *Joint Declaration on Justification*: A Case Study in Ecumenical Reception," in *Agapè: Études en l'honneur de Mgr. Pierre Duprey, M. Afr.,* ed. Jean-Marie Roger Tillard, OP (Chambésy-Genève: Centre Orthodoxe du Patriarcat Oecuménique, 2000), 169–84.

27. On some of the limitations of *From Conflict to Communion*, see U. Körtner, "Une raison pour féter et non se lamenter: Remarques sur le point de vue luthéro-catholique à propos du jubilee de 2017," *Istina* 58, no. 3 (2013): 263–68.

twentieth century regarding Martin Luther and the Reformation, indicating the significance of ecumenical scholarship in the presentation of a new evaluation of Luther and the sixteenth-century event.

Chapter three follows up the contents of the preceding chapter with a historical sketch of the Reformation and the Catholic response. It suggests that Lutherans and Catholics today have a common way of remembering these past events that can overcome the traditional anti-Lutheran and anti-Catholic interpretations of yesteryear. The chapter is largely a historical overview, although it acknowledges that it does not offer a full account of the history.

Chapter four is devoted to the basic themes of Martin Luther's theology in the light of the work of the Lutheran–Roman Catholic dialogue. It describes how these dialogues have sought to overcome some of the controversial points of Luther's theology by identifying the different terminologies, thought structures, and concerns of Luther and his Catholic opponents. The chapter validly makes two points: there is a distinction between Luther's theology and Lutheran theology, and not all points covered in the dialogue have been equally received by Catholics and Lutherans.

Chapter five addresses directly the subject of a common commemoration in 2017. It declares that baptism is the basis for both Christian unity and the common commemoration. By baptism Lutherans and Catholics, although in divided communities, belong to the one body of Christ. Both communities in the past have sinned against this unity. Both ask for God's forgiveness. The chapter closes with a mention of Lutheran contrition for Lutheran harm done to Anabaptists in the sixteenth century. It is one of the few references to other Reformation groups in *From Conflict to Communion*.

Chapter six offers to readers five ecumenical imperatives to be utilized by Lutherans and Catholics in regard to the upcoming commemoration:

(1) Catholics and Lutherans should always begin from the perspective of unity and not of division.
(2) Catholics and Lutherans must let themselves be transformed by the encounter with the other and by the mutual witness of both.
(3) Lutherans and Catholics should commit themselves to seek visible unity, to elaborate what this means, and to strive toward the goal.
(4) Lutherans and Catholics should jointly rediscover the power of the gospel of Jesus Christ in this time.
(5) Catholics and Lutherans should witness together to the mercy of God in proclamation and service to the world.

From Conflict to Communion concludes by providing a list of all the common statements that have been produced by the international dialogue (the Lutheran–Roman Catholic Commission on Unity). This section could have been enhanced if it were a complete bibliography indicating where the reader could find these texts. The footnotes in this introduction provide such information.

The literature that has been and will be produced for the year 2017 will be voluminous and of varying quality. In that sea of writing *From Conflict to Communion* deserves special mention and attention. It originated in a group officially appointed by both the Lutheran and Roman Catholic traditions. It seeks to inform its audience concerning both the past and the present, and it seeks to offer encouragement to take concrete steps toward greater expressions of Catholic-Lutheran unity.

Thus it is critical that *From Conflict to Communion* be available to the largest readership possible. This American edition with study guide and liturgical material for joint worship seeks to meet that goal. This volume would not have been possible without the support and encouragement of William B. Eerdmans Jr., chairman of the William B. Eerdmans Publishing Company, and the Rev. Dr. Norman A. Hjelm; the permission of the Lutheran World Federation; and the permission of the Diocese of Pittsburgh of the Roman Catholic Church and the Southwestern Synod of the Evangelical Lutheran Church in America to reproduce the study guide.

Special mention and gratitude must be expressed to an anonymous supporter whose financial gift played a crucial role in making this publication possible.

From Conflict to Communion

Lutheran–Roman Catholic Common Commemoration of the Reformation in 2017

Report of the Lutheran–Roman Catholic Commission on Unity

Foreword

Martin Luther's struggle with God drove and defined his whole life. The question, How can I find a gracious God? plagued him constantly. He found the gracious God in the gospel of Jesus Christ. "True theology and the knowledge of God are in the crucified Christ."

In 2017, Catholic and Lutheran Christians will most fittingly look back on events that occurred 500 years earlier by putting the gospel of Jesus Christ at the center. The gospel should be celebrated and communicated to the people of our time so that the world may believe that God gives Himself to human beings and calls us into communion with Himself and His church. Herein lies the basis for our joy in our common faith.

To this joy also belongs a discerning, self-critical look at ourselves, not only in our history, but also today. We Christians have certainly not always been faithful to the gospel; all too often we have conformed ourselves to the thought and behavioral patterns of the surrounding world. Repeatedly, we have stood in the way of the good news of the mercy of God.

Both as individuals and as a community of believers, we all constantly require repentance and reform—encouraged and led by the Holy Spirit. "When our Lord and Master, Jesus Christ, said 'Repent,' He called for the entire life of believers to be one of repentance." Thus reads the opening statement of Luther's 95 Theses from 1517, which triggered the Reformation movement.

Although this thesis is anything but self-evident today, we Lutheran and Catholic Christians want to take it seriously by directing our critical glance first at ourselves and not at each other. We take as our guiding rule the doctrine of justification, which expresses the message of the gospel and therefore "constantly serves to orient all the teaching and practice of our churches to Christ" (*Joint Declaration on the Doctrine of Justification*).

The true unity of the church can only exist as unity in the truth of the gospel of Jesus Christ. The fact that the struggle for this truth in the sixteenth century led to the loss of unity in Western Christendom belongs to the dark pages of church history. In 2017, we must confess openly that we have been guilty before Christ of damaging the unity of the church. This commemorative year presents us with two challenges: the purification and healing of memories, and the restoration of Christian unity in accordance with the truth of the gospel of Jesus Christ (Eph 4:4–6).

The following text describes a way "from conflict to communion"—a way whose goal we have not yet reached. Nevertheless, the Lutheran–Roman Catholic Commission for Unity has taken seriously the words of Pope John XXIII, "The things that unite us are greater than those that divide us."

We invite all Christians to study the report of our Commission both open-mindedly and critically, and to come with us along the way to a deeper communion of all Christians.

KARLHEINZ DIEZ
Auxiliary Bishop of Fulda
(on behalf of the Catholic co-chair)

EERO HUOVINEN
Bishop Emeritus of Helsinki
Lutheran co-chair

Introduction

1. In 2017, Lutheran and Catholic Christians will commemorate together the 500th anniversary of the beginning of the Reformation. Lutherans and Catholics today enjoy a growth in mutual understanding, cooperation, and respect. They have come to acknowledge that more unites than divides them: above all, common faith in the Triune God and the revelation in Jesus Christ, as well as recognition of the basic truths of the doctrine of justification.

2. Already the 450th anniversary of the Augsburg Confession in 1980 offered both Lutherans and Catholics the opportunity to develop a common understanding of the foundational truths of the faith by pointing to Jesus Christ as the living center of our Christian faith.[1] On the 500th anniversary of Martin Luther's birth in 1983, the international dialogue between Roman Catholics and Lutherans jointly affirmed a number of Luther's essential concerns. The commission's report designated him "Witness to Jesus Christ" and declared, "Christians, whether Protestant or Catholic, cannot disregard the person and the message of this man."[2]

3. The upcoming year of 2017 challenges Catholics and Lutherans to discuss in dialogue the issues and consequences of the Wittenberg

---

1. Roman Catholic/Lutheran Joint Commission, "All under One Christ: Statement on the Augsburg Confession 1980," in Harding Meyer and Lucas Visher (eds), *Growth in Agreement I: Reports and Agreed Statements of Ecumenical Conversations on a World Level, 1972–1982* (Geneva: World Council of Churches, 1984), 241–47.

2. Roman Catholic/Lutheran Joint Commission, "Martin Luther: Witness to Jesus Christ" I.1, in Jeffrey Gros, FSC, Harding Meyer and William G. Rusch (eds), *Growth in Agreement II: Reports and Agreed Statements of Ecumenical Conversations on a World Level, 1982–1998* (Geneva: WCC Publications, 2000), 438.

Reformation, which centered on the person and thought of Martin Luther, and to develop perspectives for the remembrance and appropriation of the Reformation today. Luther's reforming agenda poses a spiritual and theological challenge for both contemporary Catholics and Lutherans.

CHAPTER I

Commemorating the Reformation
in an Ecumenical and Global Age

4. Every commemoration has its own context. Today, the context includes three main challenges, which present both opportunities and obligations: (1) It is the first commemoration to take place during the ecumenical age. Therefore, the common commemoration is an occasion to deepen communion between Catholics and Lutherans. (2) It is the first commemoration in the age of globalization. Therefore, the common commemoration must incorporate the experiences and perspectives of Christians from South and North, East and West. (3) It is the first commemoration that must deal with the necessity of a new evangelization in a time marked by both the proliferation of new religious movements and, at the same time, the growth of secularization in many places. Therefore, the common commemoration has the opportunity and obligation to be a common witness of faith.

THE CHARACTER OF PREVIOUS COMMEMORATIONS

5. Relatively early, 31 October 1517 became a symbol of the sixteenth-century Protestant Reformation. Still today, many Lutheran churches remember each year on 31 October the event known as "the Reformation." The centennial celebrations of the Reformation have been lavish and festive. The opposing viewpoints of the different confessional groups have been especially visible at these events. For Lutherans, these commemorative days and centennials were occasions for telling once again the story of the beginning of the characteristic—"evangelical"— form of their church in order to justify their distinctive existence. This was naturally tied to a critique of the Roman Catholic Church. On the

other side, Catholics took such commemorative events as opportunities to accuse Lutherans of an unjustifiable division from the true church and a rejection of the gospel of Christ.

6. Political and church-political agendas frequently shaped these earlier centenary commemorations. In 1617, for example, the observance of the 100th anniversary helped to stabilize and revitalize the common Reformation identity of Lutherans and Reformed at their joint commemorative celebrations. Lutherans and Reformed demonstrated their solidarity through strong polemics against the Roman Catholic Church. Together they celebrated Luther as the liberator from the Roman yoke. Much later, in 1917, amidst the First World War, Luther was portrayed as a German national hero.

THE FIRST ECUMENICAL COMMEMORATION

7. The year 2017 will see the first centennial commemoration of the Reformation to take place during the ecumenical age. It will also mark fifty years of Lutheran–Roman Catholic dialogue. As part of the ecumenical movement, praying together, worshipping together, and serving their communities together have enriched Catholics and Lutherans. They also face political, social, and economic challenges together. The spirituality evident in interconfessional marriages has brought forth new insights and questions. Lutherans and Catholics have been able to reinterpret their theological traditions and practices, recognizing the influences they have had on each other. Therefore, they long to commemorate 2017 together.

8. These changes demand a new approach. It is no longer adequate simply to repeat earlier accounts of the Reformation period, which presented Lutheran and Catholic perspectives separately and often in opposition to one another. Historical remembrance always selects from among a great abundance of historical moments and assimilates the selected elements into a meaningful whole. Because these accounts of the past were mostly oppositional, they not infrequently intensified the conflict between the confessions and sometimes led to open hostility.

9. The historical remembrance has had material consequences for the relationship of the confessions to each other. For this reason, a common ecumenical remembrance of the Lutheran Reformation is both so important and at the same time so difficult. Even today, many Catholics

associate the word "Reformation" first of all with the division of the church, while many Lutheran Christians associate the word "Reformation" chiefly with the rediscovery of the gospel, certainty of faith and freedom. It will be necessary to take both points of departure seriously in order to relate the two perspectives to each other and bring them into dialogue.

COMMEMORATION IN A NEW GLOBAL AND SECULAR CONTEXT

10. In the last century, Christianity has become increasingly global. There are today Christians of various confessions throughout the whole world; the number of Christians in the South is growing, while the number of Christians in the North is shrinking. The churches of the South are continually assuming a greater importance within worldwide Christianity. These churches do not easily see the confessional conflicts of the sixteenth century as their own conflicts, even if they are connected to the churches of Europe and North America through various Christian world communions and share with them a common doctrinal basis. With regard to the year 2017, it will be very important to take seriously the contributions, questions, and perspectives of these churches.

11. In lands where Christianity has already been at home for many centuries, many people have left the churches in recent times or have forgotten their ecclesial traditions. In these traditions, churches have handed on from generation to generation what they had received from their encounter with the Holy Scripture: an understanding of God, humanity, and the world in response to the revelation of God in Jesus Christ; the wisdom developed over the course of generations from the experience of lifelong engagement of Christians with God; and the treasury of liturgical forms, hymns and prayers, catechetical practices, and diaconal services. As a result of this forgetting, much of what divided the church in the past is virtually unknown today.

12. Ecumenism, however, cannot base itself on forgetfulness of tradition. But how, then, will the history of the Reformation be remembered in 2017? What of that which the two confessions fought over in the sixteenth century deserves to be preserved? Our fathers and mothers in the faith were convinced that there was something worth fighting for, something that was necessary for a life with God. How can the

often forgotten traditions be handed on to our contemporaries so as not to remain objects of antiquarian interest only, but rather support a vibrant Christian existence? How can the traditions be passed on in such a way that they do not dig new trenches between Christians of different confessions?

NEW CHALLENGES FOR THE 2017 COMMEMORATION

13. Over the centuries, church and culture often have been interwoven in the most intimate way possible. Much that has belonged to the life of the church has, over the course of centuries, also found a place in the cultures of those countries and plays a role in them even to this day, even at times independently of the churches. The preparations for 2017 will need to identify these various elements of the tradition now present in the culture, to interpret them, and to lead a conversation between church and culture in light of these different aspects.

14. For more than a hundred years, Pentecostal and other charismatic movements have become very widespread across the globe. These powerful movements have put forward new emphases that have made many of the old confessional controversies seem obsolete. The Pentecostal movement is present in many other churches in the form of the charismatic movement, creating new commonalities and communities across confessional boundaries. Thus, this movement opens up new ecumenical opportunities while, at the same time, creating additional challenges that will play a significant role in the observance of the Reformation in 2017.

15. While the previous Reformation anniversaries took place in confessionally homogenous lands, or lands at least where a majority of the population was Christian, today Christians live worldwide in multi-religious environments. This pluralism poses a new challenge for ecumenism, making ecumenism not superfluous but, on the contrary, all the more urgent, since the animosity of confessional oppositions harms Christian credibility. How Christians deal with differences among themselves can reveal something about their faith to people of other religions. Because the question of how to handle inner-Christian conflict is especially acute on the occasion of remembering the beginning of the Reformation, this aspect of the changed situation deserves special attention in our reflections on the year 2017.

CHAPTER II

New Perspectives on Martin Luther and the Reformation

16. What happened in the past cannot be changed, but what is remembered of the past and how it is remembered can, with the passage of time, indeed change. Remembrance makes the past present. While the past itself is unalterable, the presence of the past in the present is alterable. In view of 2017, the point is not to tell a different history, but to tell that history differently.

17. Lutherans and Catholics have many reasons to retell their history in new ways. They have been brought closer together through family relations, through their service to the larger world mission, and through their common resistance to tyrannies in many places. These deepened contacts have changed mutual perceptions, bringing new urgency for ecumenical dialogue and further research. The ecumenical movement has altered the orientation of the churches' perceptions of the Reformation: ecumenical theologians have decided not to pursue their confessional self-assertions at the expense of their dialogue partners but rather to search for that which is common within the differences, even within the oppositions, and thus work toward overcoming church-dividing differences.

CONTRIBUTIONS OF RESEARCH ON THE MIDDLE AGES

18. Research has contributed much to changing the perception of the past in a number of ways. In the case of the Reformation, these include the Protestant as well as the Catholic accounts of church history, which have been able to correct previous confessional depictions of history through strict methodological guidelines and reflection on the condi-

tions of their own points of view and presuppositions. On the Catholic side that applies especially to the newer research on Luther and the Reformation and, on the Protestant side, to an altered picture of medieval theology and to a broader and more differentiated treatment of the late Middle Ages. In current depictions of the Reformation period, there is also new attention to a vast number of non-theological factors—political, economic, social, and cultural. The paradigm of "confessionalization" has made important corrections to previous historiography of the period.

19. The late Middle Ages are no longer seen as total darkness, as often portrayed by Protestants, nor are they perceived as entirely light, as in older Catholic depictions. This age appears today as a time of great oppositions—of external piety and deep interiority; of works-oriented theology in the sense of *do ut des* ("I give you so that you give me") and conviction of one's total dependence on the grace of God; of indifference toward religious obligations, even the obligations of office, and serious reforms, as in some of the monastic orders.

20. The church was anything but a monolithic entity; the *corpus christianum* encompassed very diverse theologies, lifestyles, and conceptions of the church. Historians say that the fifteenth century was an especially pious time in the church. During this period, more and more lay people received a good education and so were eager to hear better preaching and a theology that would help them to lead Christian lives. Luther picked up on such streams of theology and piety and developed them further.

Twentieth-century Catholic research on Luther

21. Twentieth-century Catholic research on Luther built upon a Catholic interest in Reformation history that awakened in the second half of the nineteenth century. These theologians followed the efforts of the Catholic population in the Protestant-dominated German Empire to free themselves from a one-sided, anti-Roman, Protestant historiography. The breakthrough for Catholic scholarship came with the thesis that Luther overcame within himself a Catholicism that was not fully Catholic. According to this view, the life and teaching of the church in the late Middle Ages served mainly as a negative foil for the Refor-

mation; the crisis in Catholicism made Luther's religious protest quite convincing to some.

22. In a new way, Luther was portrayed as an earnest religious person and conscientious man of prayer. Painstaking and detailed historical research has demonstrated that Catholic literature on Luther over the previous four centuries right up through modernity had been significantly shaped by the commentaries of Johannes Cochaleus, a contemporary opponent of Luther and advisor to Duke George of Saxony. Cochaleus had characterized Luther as an apostatized monk, a destroyer of Christendom, a corrupter of morals, and a heretic. The achievement of this first period of critical, but sympathetic, engagement with Luther's character was the freeing of Catholic research from the one-sided approach of such polemical works on Luther. Sober historical analyses by other Catholic theologians showed that it was not the core concerns of the Reformation, such as the doctrine of justification, which led to the division of the church but, rather, Luther's criticisms of the condition of the church at his time that sprang from these concerns.

23. The next step for Catholic research on Luther was to uncover analogous contents embedded in different theological thought structures and systems, carried out especially by a systematic comparison between the exemplary theologians of the two confessions, Thomas Aquinas and Martin Luther. This work allowed theologians to understand Luther's theology within its own framework. At the same time, Catholic research examined the meaning of the doctrine of justification within the Augsburg Confession. Here Luther's reforming concerns could be set within the broader context of the composition of the Lutheran confessions, with the result that the intention of the Augsburg Confession could be seen as expressing fundamental reforming concerns as well as preserving the unity of the church.

ECUMENICAL PROJECTS PREPARING THE WAY FOR CONSENSUS

24. These efforts led directly to the ecumenical project, begun in 1980 by Lutheran and Catholic theologians in Germany on the occasion of the 450th anniversary of the presentation of the Augsburg Confession, of a Catholic recognition of the Augsburg Confession. The extensive achievements of a later ecumenical working group of Protestant and Catholic theologians, tracing its roots back to this project of Catholic

research on Luther, resulted in the study *The Condemnations of the Reformation Era: Do They Still Divide?*[1]

25. The *Joint Declaration on the Doctrine of Justification,*[2] signed by both the Lutheran World Federation and the Roman Catholic Church in 1999, built on this groundwork as well as on the work of the US dialogue *Justification by Faith,*[3] and affirmed a consensus in the basic truths of the doctrine of justification between Lutherans and Catholics.

CATHOLIC DEVELOPMENTS

26. The Second Vatican Council, responding to the scriptural, liturgical, and patristic revival of the preceding decades, dealt with such themes as esteem and reverence for the Holy Scripture in the life of the church, the rediscovery of the common priesthood of all the baptized, the need for continual purification and reform of the church, the understanding of church office as service, and the importance of the freedom and responsibility of human beings, including the recognition of religious freedom.

27. The Council also affirmed elements of sanctification and truth even outside the structures of the Roman Catholic Church. It asserted, "some and even very many of the significant elements and endowments which together go to build up and give life to the Church itself, can exist outside the visible boundaries of the Catholic Church," and it named these elements "the written word of God; the life of grace; faith, hope and charity, with the other interior gifts of the Holy Spirit, and visible elements too" (*UR* 1).[4] The Council also spoke of the "many liturgical actions of the Christian religion" that are used by the divided "brethren" and said, "these most certainly can truly engender

1. Karl Lehmann and Wolfhart Pannenberg (eds), *Condemnations of the Reformation Era: Do They Still Divide?* tr. Margaret Kohl (Minneapolis, MN: Fortress, 1990).

2. The Lutheran World Federation and the Roman Catholic Church, *Joint Declaration on the Doctrine of Justification* (Grand Rapids, MI/Cambridge, U.K.: William B. Eerdmans, 2000). Originally published as *Gemeinsame Erklärung zur Rechtfertigungslehre* (Frankfurt am Main: Verlag Otto Lembeck/Paderborn: Bonifatius-Verlag, 1999).

3. H. George Anderson, T. Austin Murphy, Joseph A. Burgess (eds), *Justification by Faith*, Lutherans and Catholics in Dialogue VII (Minneapolis, MN: Augsburg Publishing House, 1985).

4. *Unitatis Redintegratio* = *UR*.

a life of grace in ways that vary according to the condition of each Church or Community. These liturgical actions must be regarded as capable of giving access to the community of salvation" (*UR* 3). The acknowledgement extended not only to the individual elements and actions in these communities, but also to the "divided churches and communities" themselves. "For the Spirit of Christ has not refrained from using them as means of salvation" (*UR* 1.3).

28. In light of the renewal of Catholic theology evident in the Second Vatican Council, Catholics today can appreciate Martin Luther's reforming concerns and regard them with more openness than seemed possible earlier.

29. Implicit rapprochement with Luther's concerns has led to a new evaluation of his catholicity, which took place in the context of recognizing that his intention was to reform, not to divide, the church. This is evident in the statements of Johannes Cardinal Willebrands and Pope John Paul II.[5] The rediscovery of these two central characteristics of his person and theology led to a new ecumenical understanding of Luther as a "witness to the gospel."

30. Pope Benedict also recognized the ways in which the person and theology of Martin Luther pose a spiritual and theological challenge to Catholic theology today when, in 2011, he visited the Augustinian Friary in Erfurt where Luther had lived as a friar for about six years. Pope Benedict commented, "What constantly exercised [Luther] was the question of God, the deep passion and driving force of his whole life's journey. 'How do I find a gracious God?'—this question struck him in the heart and lay at the foundation of all his theological searching and inner struggle. For him, theology was no mere academic pursuit, but the struggle for oneself, which in turn was a struggle for and with God. 'How do I find a gracious God?' The fact that this question was the driving force of his whole life never ceases to make an impression on me. For who is actually concerned about this today—even among Christians? What does the question of God mean in our lives? In our preaching? Most people today, even Christians, set out from the presupposition that God is not fundamentally interested in our sins and virtues."[6]

5. Jan Willebrands, "Lecture to the 5th Assembly of the Lutheran World Federation, on July 15, 1970," in *La Documentation Catholique* (6 September 1970), 766; John Paul II, "Letter to Cardinal Willebrands for the Fifth Centenary of the Birth of Martin Luther," in *Information Service*, no. 52 (1983/II), 83–84.

6. Benedict XVI, "Address," Meeting with the Council of the Evangelical Church in

LUTHERAN DEVELOPMENTS

31. Lutheran research on Luther and the Reformation also underwent considerable development. The experiences of two world wars broke down assumptions about the progress of history and the relationship between Christianity and Western culture, while the rise of kerygmatic theology opened a new avenue for thinking about Luther. Dialogue with historians helped to integrate historical and social factors into descriptions of Reformation movements. Lutheran theologians recognized the entanglements of theological insights and political interests not only on the part of Catholics, but also on their own side. Dialogue with Catholic theologians helped them to overcome one-sided confessional approaches and to become more self-critical about aspects of their own traditions.

THE IMPORTANCE OF ECUMENICAL DIALOGUES

32. The dialogue partners are committed to the doctrines of their respective churches, which, according to their own convictions, express the truth of the faith. The doctrines demonstrate great commonalities but may differ, or even be opposed, in their formulations. Because of the former, dialogue is possible; because of the latter, dialogue is necessary.

33. Dialogue demonstrates that the partners speak different languages and understand the meanings of words differently; they make different distinctions and think in different thought forms. However, what appears to be an opposition in expression is not always an opposition in substance. In order to determine the exact relationship between respective articles of doctrine, texts must be interpreted in the light of the historical context in which they arose. That allows one to see where a difference or opposition truly exists and where it does not.

34. Ecumenical dialogue means being converted from patterns of thought that arise from and emphasize the differences between the confessions. Instead, in dialogue the partners look first for what they have in com-

---

Germany, 23 September 2011, at www.vatican.va/holy_father/benedict_xvi/speeches/2011/ september/documents/hf_ben-xvi_spe_20110923_evangelical-church-erfurt_en.html; translation altered.

mon and only then weigh the significance of their differences. These differences, however, are not overlooked or treated casually, for ecumenical dialogue is the common search for the truth of the Christian faith.

CHAPTER III

A Historical Sketch of the Lutheran Reformation and the Catholic Response

35. Today we are able to tell the story of the Lutheran Reformation together. Even though Lutherans and Catholics have different points of view, because of ecumenical dialogue they are able to overcome traditional anti-Protestant and anti-Catholic hermeneutics in order to find a common way of remembering past events. The following chapter is not a full description of the entire history and all the disputed theological points. It highlights only some of the most important historical situations and theological issues of the Reformation in the sixteenth century.

WHAT DOES REFORMATION MEAN?

36. In antiquity, the Latin noun *reformatio* referred to the idea of changing a bad present situation by returning to the good and better times of the past. In the Middle Ages, the concept of *reformatio* was very often used in the context of monastic reform. The monastic orders engaged in **reformation** in order to overcome the decline of discipline and religious lifestyle. One of the greatest reform movements originated in the tenth century in the Abbey of Cluny.

37. In the late Middle Ages, the concept of the necessity of reform was applied to the whole church. The church councils and nearly every diet of the Holy Roman Empire were concerned with *reformatio*. The Council of Constance (1414–1418) regarded the reform of the church "in head and members" as necessary.[1] A widely disseminated reform document entitled "Reformacion keyser Sigmunds" called for the restoration of

1. Council of Constance, session 3, 26 March 1415.

right order in almost every area of life. At the end of the fifteenth century, the idea of reformation also spread to the government and university.[2]

38. Luther himself seldom used the concept of "reformation." In his "Explanations of the Ninety-five Theses," Luther states, "The church needs a reformation which is not the work of man, namely the pope, or of many men, namely the cardinals, both of which the most recent council has demonstrated, but it is the work of the whole world, indeed it is the work of God alone. However, only God who has created time knows the time for this reformation."[3] Sometimes Luther used the word "reformation" in order to describe improvements of order, for example of the universities. In his reform treatise "Address to the Christian Nobility" of 1520, he called for "a just, free council" that would allow the proposals for reform to be debated.[4]

39. The term "Reformation" came to be used as a designation for the complex of historical events that, in the narrower sense, encompass the years 1517 to 1555, thus from the time of the spread of Martin Luther's "Ninety-five Theses" up until the Peace of Augsburg. The theological and ecclesiastical controversy that Luther's theology had triggered quickly became entangled with politics, the economy, and culture, due to the situation at the time. What is designated by the term "Reformation" thus reaches far beyond what Luther himself taught and intended. The concept of "Reformation" as a designation of an entire epoch comes from Leopold von Ranke who, in the nineteenth century, popularized the custom of speaking of an "age of Reformation."

REFORMATION FLASHPOINT: CONTROVERSY OVER INDULGENCES

40. On October 31, 1517, Luther sent his "Ninety-five Theses," titled, "Disputation on the Efficacy and Power of Indulgences," as an appendix

2. See the Lutheran World Federation and Pontifical Council for Promoting Christian Unity, *The Apostolicity of the Church: Study Document of the Lutheran–Roman Catholic Commission on Unity* (Minneapolis, MN: Lutheran University Press, 2006), 92, n. 8 [= *ApC*].

3. Martin Luther, "Explanations of the Ninety-Five Theses," tr. Carl W. Folkemer, in Helmut T. Lehmann and Jaroslav Pelikan (eds), *Luther's Works*, American Edition, 55 vols. (Philadelphia and St. Louis, 1955–1986), 31:250 (= *LW*); WA 1, 62, 27–31.

4. Luther, "To the Christian Nobility of the German Nation concerning the Reform of the Christian Estate," tr. Charles M. Jacobs, rev. James Atkinson, in *LW* 44:127; WA 6, 407, 1.

to a letter to Archbishop Albrecht of Mainz. In this letter, Luther expressed serious concerns about preaching and the practice of indulgences occurring under the responsibility of the Archbishop and urged him to make changes. On the same day, he wrote another letter to his Diocesan Bishop Hieronymus of Brandenburg. When Luther sent his theses to a few colleagues and most likely posted them on the door of the castle church in Wittenberg, he wished to inaugurate an academic disputation on open and unresolved questions regarding the theory and practice of indulgences.

41. Indulgences played an important role in the piety of the time. An indulgence was understood as a remission of temporal punishment due to sins whose guilt had already been forgiven. Christians could receive an indulgence under certain prescribed conditions—such as prayer, acts of charity, and almsgiving—through the action of the church, which was thought to dispense and apply the treasury of the satisfactions of Christ and the saints to penitents.

42. In Luther's opinion, the practice of indulgences damaged Christian spirituality. He questioned whether indulgences could free the penitents from penalties imposed by God; whether any penalties imposed by priests would be transferred into purgatory; whether the medicinal and purifying purpose of penalties meant that a sincere penitent would prefer to suffer the penalties instead of being liberated from them; and whether the money given for indulgences should instead be given to the poor. He also wondered about the nature of the treasury of the church out of which the pope offered indulgences.

LUTHER ON TRIAL

43. Luther's "Ninety-five Theses" spread very swiftly throughout Germany and caused a great sensation while also doing serious damage to the indulgence campaigns. Soon it was rumored that Luther would be accused of heresy. Already in December 1517, the Archbishop of Mainz had sent the "Ninety-five Theses" to Rome together with some additional material for an examination of Luther's theology.

44. Luther was surprised by the reaction to his theses, as he had not planned a public event but rather an academic disputation. He feared that the theses would be easily misunderstood if read by a wider audience. Thus, in late March 1518, he published a vernacular sermon,

"On Indulgence and Grace" ("Sermo von Ablass und Gnade"). It was an extraordinarily successful pamphlet that quickly made Luther a figure well known to the German public. Luther repeatedly insisted that, apart from the first four propositions, the theses were not his own definitive assertions but rather propositions written for disputation.

45. Rome was concerned that Luther's teaching undermined the doctrine of the church and the authority of the pope. Thus, Luther was called to Rome in order to answer to the curial court for his theology. However, upon the request of the Electoral Prince of Saxony, Frederick the Wise, the trial was transferred to Germany, to the Imperial Diet at Augsburg, where Cardinal Cajetan was given the mandate to interrogate Luther. The papal mandate said that either Luther was to recant or, in the event that Luther refused, the Cardinal had the power to ban Luther immediately or to arrest him and bring him to Rome. After the meeting, Cajetan drafted a statement for the magisterium, and the pope promulgated it soon after the interrogation in Augsburg without any response to Luther's arguments.[5]

46. A fundamental ambivalence persisted throughout the whole process leading up to Luther's excommunication. Luther offered questions for disputation and put forward arguments. He and the public, informed through many pamphlets and publications about his position and the ongoing process, expected an exchange of arguments. Luther was promised a fair trial. Nevertheless, although he was assured that he would be heard, he repeatedly received the message that he either had to recant or be proclaimed a heretic.

47. On 13 October 1518, in a solemn *protestatio*, Luther claimed that he was in agreement with the Holy Roman Church and that he could not recant unless he were convinced that he was wrong. On 22 October, he again insisted that he thought and taught within the scope of the Roman Church's teaching.

FAILED ENCOUNTERS

48. Before his encounter with Luther, Cardinal Cajetan had studied the Wittenberg professor's writings very carefully and had even written treatises on them. But Cajetan interpreted Luther within his own con-

---

5. Leo X, *Cum postquam*, 9 November 1518, *DH* 1448, cf. 1467 and 2641.

ceptual framework and thus misunderstood him on the assurance of faith, even while correctly representing the details of his position. For his part, Luther was not familiar with the cardinal's theology, and the interrogation, which allowed only for limited discussion, pressured Luther to recant. It did not provide an opportunity for Luther to understand the cardinal's position. It is a tragedy that two of the most outstanding theologians of the sixteenth century encountered one another in a trial of heresy.

49. In the following years, Luther's theology developed rapidly, giving rise to new topics of controversy. The accused theologian worked to defend his position and to gain allies in the struggle with those who were about to declare him a heretic. Many publications both for and against Luther appeared, but there was only one disputation, in 1519, in Leipzig between Andreas Bodenstein von Karlstadt and Luther on the one side, and Johannes Eck, on the other.

THE CONDEMNATION OF MARTIN LUTHER

50. Meanwhile, in Rome, the process against Luther continued and, eventually, Pope Leo X decided to act. To fulfill his "pastoral office," Pope Leo X felt obliged to protect the "orthodox faith" from those who "twist and adulterate the Scriptures" so that they are "no longer the Gospel of Christ."[6] Thus the pope issued the bull *Exsurge Domine* (15 June 1520), which condemned forty-one propositions drawn from various publications by Luther. Although they can all be found in Luther's writings and are quoted correctly, they are taken out of their respective contexts. *Exsurge Domine* describes these propositions as "heretical or scandalous, or false, or offensive to pious ears, or dangerous to simple minds, or subversive to catholic truth,"[7] without specifying which qualification applies to which proposition. At the end of the bull, the pope expressed frustration that Luther had failed to respond to any of his overtures for discussion, although he remained hopeful that Luther would experience conversion of heart and turn away from his errors.

---

6. Peter Fabisch and Erwin Iserloh (eds), *Exsurge Domine* in *Dokumente zur Causa Lutheri (1517-1521)*, vol. 2 (Münster: Aschendorffsche, 1991), 366; *Exsurge Domine*, DH 1467–1472, also at www.ewtn.com/library/papaldoc/l10exdom.htm.

7. Fabisch and Iserloh, *Exsurge Domine*, 368.

Pope Leo gave Luther sixty days either to recant his "errors" or face excommunication.

51. Eck and Aleander, who publicized *Exsurge Domine* in Germany, called for Luther's works to be burned. In response, on 10 December 1520, some Wittenberg theologians burned some books, equivalent to what would later be known as "canon law" books, along with some books of Luther's opponents, and Luther put the papal bull into the fire. Thus, it was clear that Luther was not prepared to recant. Luther was excommunicated by the bull *Decet Romanum Pontificem* on 3 January 1521.

THE AUTHORITY OF SCRIPTURE

52. The conflict concerning indulgences quickly developed into a conflict concerning authority. For Luther, the Roman curia had lost its authority by insisting only formally on its own authority instead of arguing biblically. At the beginning of the struggle, the theological authorities of Scripture, the church fathers, and the canonical tradition represented a unity for Luther. In the course of the conflict, this unity broke apart when Luther concluded that the canons as interpreted by Roman officials conflicted with Scripture. From the Catholic side, the argument was not so much about the supremacy of Scripture, with which Catholics agreed, but rather the proper interpretation of Scripture.

53. When Luther did not see a biblical basis in Rome's statements, or thought that they even contradicted the biblical message, he began to think of the pope as the Antichrist. By this, admittedly shocking, accusation, Luther meant that the pope did not allow Christ to say what Christ wanted to say and that the pope had put himself above the Bible rather than submitting to its authority. The pope claimed that his office was instituted *iure divino* ("by divine right"), while Luther could not find biblical evidence for this claim.

LUTHER IN WORMS

54. According to the laws of the Holy Roman Empire of the German Nation, a person who was excommunicated also had to be put under imperial ban. Nevertheless, the members of the Diet of Worms required that an independent authority interrogate Luther. Thus, Luther

was called to Worms and the Emperor offered Luther, now a declared heretic, a safe passage to the city. Luther had expected a disputation at the Diet, but was only asked whether he had written certain books on a table in front of him, and whether he was prepared to recant.

55. Luther responded to this invitation to recant with the famous words: "Unless I am convinced by the testimony of the Scriptures or by clear reason (for I do not trust either in the pope or in councils alone, since it is well known that they have often erred and contradicted themselves), I am bound by the Scriptures I have quoted, and my conscience is captive to the Words of God. I cannot and I will not retract anything, since it is neither safe nor right to go against conscience. May God help me. Amen."[8]

56. In response, Emperor Charles V delivered a remarkable speech in which he set forth his intentions. The emperor noted that he had descended from a long line of sovereigns who had had always considered it their duty to defend the Catholic faith "for the salvation of souls" and that he had the same duty. The emperor argued that a single friar erred when his opinion was in opposition to all of Christianity for the last thousand years.[9]

57. The Diet of Worms made Luther an outlaw who had to be arrested or even killed and commanded the rulers to suppress the "Lutheran heresy" by any means. Since Luther's argument was convincing to many of the princes and towns, they did not carry out the mandate.

Beginnings of the Reformation movement

58. Luther's understanding of the gospel was persuasive to an increasing number of priests, monks, and preachers who tried to incorporate this understanding into their preaching. Visible signs of the changes taking place were that lay people received communion under both species, some priests and monks were marrying, certain rules of fasting were no longer observed, and disrespect was at times shown to images and relics.

8. Luther, "Luther at the Diet of Worms," tr. Roger A. Hornsby, in *LW* 32:112–13. For "Words" in place of "Word," see *WA* 8, 838, 7; for omission of "I cannot do otherwise, here I stand" (cf. *WA* 8, 838, 9), see 113, n. 2: "These words are given in German in the Latin text upon which this translation is based," but "there is good evidence" that Luther did not say them.

9. Fritz Reuter (ed.), *Der Reichstag zu Worms von 1521: Reichspolitik und Luthersache*, vol. 2 (Köln and Wien: Böhlau, 1981), 226–29; see also *LW* 32, 114–15, n. 9.

59. Luther had no intention of establishing a new church, but was part of a broad and many-faceted desire for reform. He played an increasingly active role, attempting to contribute to a reform of practices and doctrines that seemed to be based on human authority alone and to be in tension with or contradiction to the Scriptures. In his treatise "To the German Nobility" (1520), Luther argued for the priesthood of all baptized and thus for an active role of the laity in church reform. Lay people played an important role in the Reformation movement, either as princes, magistrates, or ordinary people.

NEED FOR OVERSIGHT

60. Since there was no central plan and no central agency for organizing the reforms, the situation differed from town to town and village to village. A need arose to organize church visitations. As this required the authority of princes or magistrates, the reformers asked the Electoral Prince of Saxony to establish and authorize a visitation commission in 1527. Its tasks were not only to evaluate the preaching and the whole service and life of the ministers, but also to ensure that they received resources for their personal sustenance.

61. The commission installed something like a church government. The superintendents were charged with the task of overseeing the ministers of a certain region and supervising their doctrine and way of life. The commission also examined the orders of service and oversaw the unity of these orders. In 1528, a ministers' handbook was published that addressed all their major doctrinal and practical problems. It played an important role in the history of the Lutheran doctrinal confessions.

BRINGING THE SCRIPTURE TO THE PEOPLE

62. Luther, together with colleagues at the University of Wittenberg, translated the Bible into German so that more people were able to read it for themselves and, among other uses, to engage in spiritual and theological discernment for their life in the church. For that reason, Lutheran reformers established schools for both boys and girls and made serious efforts to convince parents to send their children to school.

CATECHISMS AND HYMNS

63. In order to improve the poor knowledge of the Christian faith among ministers and lay people, Luther wrote his Small Catechism for a general audience and the Large Catechism for pastors and well-educated laity. The catechisms explained the Ten Commandments, the Lord's Prayer, and the creeds, and included sections on the sacraments of Holy baptism and the Holy Supper. The Small Catechism, Luther's most influential book, greatly enhanced the knowledge of faith among ordinary people.

64. These catechisms were intended to help people live a Christian life and to gain the capacity for theological and spiritual discernment. The catechisms illustrate the fact that, for the reformers, faith meant not only trusting in Christ and his promise, but also affirming the propositional content of faith that can and must be learned.

65. To promote lay participation in the services, the reformers wrote hymns and published hymnbooks. These played an enduring role in Lutheran spirituality and became part of the treasured heritage of the whole church.

MINISTERS FOR THE PARISHES

66. Now that the Lutheran parishes had the Scriptures in the vernacular, the catechism, hymns, a church order, and orders of service, a major problem remained, namely how to provide ministers for the parishes. During the first years of the Reformation, many priests and monks became Lutheran ministers, so that enough pastors were available. But this method of recruiting ministers eventually proved to be insufficient.

67. It is remarkable that the reformers waited until 1535 before they organized their own ordinations in Wittenberg. In the Augsburg Confession (1530), the reformers declared that they were prepared to obey the bishops if the bishops themselves would allow the preaching of the gospel according to Reformation beliefs. Since this did not happen, the reformers had to choose between maintaining the traditional way of ordaining priests by bishops, thereby giving up Reformation preaching, or keeping Reformation preaching, but ordaining pastors by other pastors. The reformers chose the second solution, reclaiming a

tradition of interpreting the Pastoral Epistles that went back to Jerome in the early church.

68. Members of the Wittenberg theological faculty, acting on behalf of the church, examined both the doctrine and the lives of the candidates. Ordinations took place in Wittenberg rather than in the parishes of the ordinands, since the ministers were ordained to the ministry of the entire church. The ordination testimonies emphasized the ordinands' doctrinal agreement with the catholic church. The ordination rite consisted in the laying on of hands and prayer to the Holy Spirit.

THEOLOGICAL ATTEMPTS TO OVERCOME THE RELIGIOUS CONFLICT

69. The Augsburg Confession (1530) attempted to settle the religious conflict of the Lutheran Reformation. Its first part (articles 1–21) presents Lutheran teaching held to be in agreement with the doctrine of "the catholic church, or from the Roman church";[10] its second part deals with changes that the reformers initiated to correct certain practices understood as "misuses" (articles 22–28), giving reasons for changing these practices. The end of part 1 reads, "This is a nearly complete summary of the teaching among us. As can be seen, there is nothing here that departs from the Scriptures or the catholic church, or from the Roman church, insofar as we can tell from its writers. Because this is so, those who claim that our people are to be regarded as heretics judge too harshly."[11]

70. The Augsburg Confession is a strong testimony to the Lutheran reformers' resolve to maintain the unity of the church and remain within one visible church. In explicitly presenting the difference as of only minor significance, it is similar to what we today would call a differentiating consensus.

71. Immediately, some Catholic theologians saw the need to respond to the Augsburg Confession and quickly produced the Confutation of the Augsburg Confession. This Confutation closely followed the text and

10. "The Augsburg Confession," Latin text, in Robert Kolb and Timothy J. Wengert (eds), *The Book of Concord: The Confessions of the Evangelical Lutheran Church* (Minneapolis, MN: Fortress, 2000), 59.

11. Ibid.

arguments of the Confession. The Confutation was able to affirm along with the Augsburg Confession a number of core Christian teachings such as the doctrines of the Trinity, Christ, and baptism. The Confutation, however, rejected a number of Lutheran teachings on the doctrines of the church and sacraments on the basis of biblical and patristic texts. Since Lutherans could not be persuaded by the Confutation's arguments, an official dialogue was initiated in late August 1530 in order to reconcile the differences between the Confession and the Confutation. This dialogue, however, was unable to resolve the remaining ecclesiological and sacramental problems.

72. Another attempt to overcome the religious conflict was the so-called *Religionsgespräche* or Colloquies (Speyer/Hagenau [1540], Worms [1540–1541], Regensburg [1541–1546]). The Emperor or his brother, King Ferdinand, convened the conversations, which took place under the leadership of an imperial representative. The goal was to persuade the Lutherans to return to the convictions of their opponents. Tactics, intrigues, and political pressure played an important role in them.

73. The negotiators achieved a remarkable text on the doctrine of justification in the *Regensburger Buch* (1541), but the conflict concerning the doctrine of the eucharist seemed to be insurmountable. In the end, both Rome and Luther rejected the results, leading to the ultimate failure of these negotiations.

RELIGIOUS WAR AND THE PEACE OF AUGSBURG

74. The Smalcald War (1546–1547) of Emperor Charles V against the Lutheran territories aimed at defeating the princes and forcing them to revoke all changes. In the beginning the Emperor was successful. He won the war (20 July 1547). His troops were soon in Wittenberg where the Emperor hindered the soldiers from exhuming Luther's body and burning it.

75. At the Diet in Augsburg (1547–1548), the Emperor imposed the so-called Augsburg Interim on the Lutherans, leading to endless conflicts in Lutheran territories. This document explained justification mainly as grace that stimulates love. It emphasized subordination under the bishops and the pope. However, it also permitted the marriage of priests and communion under both species.

76. In 1552, after a conspiracy of princes, a new war against the Emperor

began that forced him to flee from Austria. This led to a peace treaty between Lutheran princes and King Ferdinand. Thus, the attempt to eradicate "the Lutheran heresy" through military means ultimately failed.

77. The war ended with the Peace of Augsburg in 1555. This treaty was an attempt to find ways for people of different religious convictions to live together in one country. Territories and towns that adhered to the Augsburg Confession as well as Catholic territories were recognized in the German Empire, but not people of other beliefs, such as the Reformed and the Anabaptists. The princes and magistrates had the right to determine the religion of their subjects. If the prince changed his religion, the people living in the territory would also have to change theirs, except in the areas where bishops were princes (*geistliche Fürstentümer*). The subjects had the right to emigrate if they did not agree with the religion of the prince.

THE COUNCIL OF TRENT

78. The Council of Trent (1545–1563), convened a generation after Luther's reform, began before the Smalcald War (1546–1547) and ended after the Peace of Augsburg (1555). The bull *Laetare Jerusalem* (19 November 1544) set three orders of business for the Council: healing of the confessional split, reforming the church, and establishing peace so that a defense against the Ottomans could be elaborated.

79. The Council decided that at each session there would be a dogmatic decree, affirming the faith of the church, and a disciplinary decree helping to reform the church. For the most part, the dogmatic decrees did not present a comprehensive theological account of the faith, but rather concentrated on those doctrines disputed by the reformers in a way that emphasized points of difference.

Scripture and tradition

80. The Council, wishing to preserve the "purity of the gospel purged of all errors," approved its decree on the sources of revelation on 8 April 1546. Without explicitly naming it, the Council rejected the principle of *sola scriptura* by arguing against the isolation of Scripture from tradition.

The Council decreed that the gospel, "the source of the whole truth of salvation and rule of conduct," was preserved "in written books and unwritten traditions," without, however, resolving the relationship between Scripture and tradition. Moreover, it taught that the apostolic traditions concerning faith and morals were "preserved in unbroken sequence in the Catholic Church." Scripture and tradition were to be accepted "with a like feeling of piety and reverence."[12]

81. The decree published a list of the canonical books of the Old and New Testaments.[13] The Council insisted that the sacred Scriptures can neither be interpreted contrary to the teaching of the church nor contrary to the "unanimous teaching of the Fathers" of the church. Finally, the Council declared that the old Latin vulgate edition of the Bible was an "authentic" text for use in the church.[14]

Justification

82. Regarding justification, the Council explicitly rejected both the Pelagian doctrine of works righteousness and the doctrine of justification by faith alone (*sola fide*), while understanding faith primarily as assent to revealed doctrine. The Council affirmed the Christological basis of justification by affirming that human beings are grafted into Christ and that the grace of Christ is necessary for the entire process of justification, although the process does not exclude dispositions for grace or the collaboration of free will. It declared the essence of justification to be not the remission of sins alone, but also the "sanctification and renovation of the inner man" by supernatural charity.[15] The formal cause of justification is "the justice of God, not that by which He Himself is just, but that by which He makes us just," and the final cause of justification is "the glory of God and of Christ and life everlasting."[16] Faith was affirmed as the "beginning, foundation and root" of justification.[17] The grace of justification can be lost by mortal sin and not only by the loss of faith,

---

12. Council of Trent, Fourth Session, 8 April 1546, Decree Concerning the Canonical Scriptures.

13. Ibid.

14. Ibid., Decree Concerning the Edition and Use of the Sacred Books.

15. Council of Trent, Sixth Session, 13 January 1547, chapter VII.

16. Ibid.

17. Ibid., chapter VIII.

although it can be regained through the sacrament of penance.[18] The Council affirmed that eternal life is a grace, not merely a reward.[19]

The sacraments

83. At its seventh session, the Council presented the sacraments as the ordinary means by which "all true justice either begins, or once received gains strength, or, if lost, is restored."[20] The Council decreed that Christ instituted seven sacraments and defined them as efficacious signs causing grace by the rite itself (*ex opere operato*) and not simply by reason of the recipient's faith.

84. The debate on communion under both species expressed the doctrine that under either species the whole and undivided Christ is received.[21] After the conclusion of the Council (16 April 1565), the pope authorized the chalice for the laity under certain conditions for several ecclesiastical provinces of Germany and the hereditary territories of the Habsburgs.

85. In response to the reformers' critique of the sacrificial character of the Mass, the Council affirmed the Mass as a propitiatory sacrifice that made present the sacrifice of the cross. The Council taught that, since in the Mass Christ the priest offers the same sacrificial gifts as on the cross, but in a different way, the Mass is not a repetition of the once-for-all sacrifice of Calvary. The Council defined that the Mass may be offered in honor of the saints and for the faithful, living and dead.[22]

86. The decree on holy orders defined the sacramental character of ordination and the existence of an ecclesiastical hierarchy based on divine ordinance.[23]

Pastoral reforms

87. The Council also initiated pastoral reforms. Its reform decrees promoted a more effective proclamation of the Word of God through

18. Ibid., chapter XIV.
19. Ibid., chapter XVI.
20. Council of Trent, Seventh Session, 3 March 1547, Foreword.
21. Council of Trent, Twenty-first Session, 16 July 1562, chapter III, can. 2.
22. Council of Trent, Twenty-second Session, 17 September 1562, chapter II, can. 3.
23. Council of Trent, Twenty-third Session, 15 July 1563, chapters III and IV.

the establishment of seminaries for the better training of priests and through the requirement of preaching on Sundays and holy days. Bishops and pastors were obliged to reside in their dioceses and parishes. The Council eliminated some abuses in matters of jurisdiction, ordination, patronage, benefices, and indulgences at the same time that it expanded episcopal powers. Bishops were empowered to make visitations of exempt parochial benefices and oversee the pastoral work of exempt orders and chapters. It provided for provincial and diocesan synods. In order better to communicate the faith, the Council encouraged the emerging practice of writing catechisms, such as those of Peter of Canisius, and made provision for the Roman Catechism.

Consequences

88. The Council of Trent, although to a large extent a response to the Protestant Reformation, did not condemn individuals or communities but specific doctrinal positions. Because the doctrinal decrees of the Council were largely in response to what it perceived to be Protestant errors, it shaped a polemical environment between Protestants and Catholics that tended to define Catholicism over and against Protestantism. In this approach, it mirrored many of the Lutheran confessional writings, which also defined Lutheran positions by opposition. The decisions of the Council of Trent laid the basis for the formation of Catholic identity up to the Second Vatican Council.

89. By the end of the third gathering of the Council of Trent, it had to be soberly acknowledged that the unity of the church in the Western world had been shattered. New church structures developed in the Lutheran territories. The Peace of Augsburg of 1555 at first secured stable political relationships, but it could not prevent the great European conflict of the seventeenth century, the Thirty Years' War (1618–1648). The establishment of secular nation-states with strong confessionalistic delineations remained a burden inherited from the Reformation period.

THE SECOND VATICAN COUNCIL

90. While the Council of Trent largely defined Catholic relations with Lutherans for several centuries, its legacy must now be viewed through

the lens of the actions of the Second Vatican Council (1962–1965). This Council made it possible for the Catholic Church to enter the ecumenical movement and leave behind the charged polemic atmosphere of the post-Reformation era. The Dogmatic Constitution on the Church (*Lumen Gentium*), the Decree on Ecumenism (*Unitatis Redintegratio*), the Declaration on Religious Freedom (*Dignitate Humanae*), and the Dogmatic Constitution on Divine Revelation (*Dei Verbum*) are foundational documents for Catholic ecumenism. Vatican II, while affirming that the Church of Christ subsists in the Catholic Church, also acknowledged, "many elements of sanctification and of truth are found outside of its visible structure. These elements, as gifts belonging to the Church of Christ, are forces impelling toward catholic unity" (*LG* 8). There was a positive appreciation of what Catholics share with other Christian churches such as the creeds, baptism, and the Scriptures. A theology of ecclesial communion affirmed that Catholics are in a real, if imperfect, communion with all who confess Jesus Christ and are baptized (*UR* 2).

CHAPTER IV

Basic Themes of Martin Luther's Theology in Light of the Lutheran–Roman Catholic Dialogues

91. Since the sixteenth century, basic convictions of both Martin Luther and Lutheran theology have been a matter of controversy between Catholics and Lutherans. Ecumenical dialogues and academic research have analyzed these controversies and attempted to overcome them by identifying the different terminologies, different thought structures, and different concerns that do not necessarily exclude each other.

92. In this chapter, Catholics and Lutherans jointly present some of the main theological affirmations developed by Martin Luther. This common description does not mean that Catholics agree with everything that Martin Luther said as presented here. An ongoing need for ecumenical dialogue and mutual understanding remains. Nevertheless, we have reached a stage in our ecumenical journey that enables us to give this common account.

93. It is important to distinguish between Luther's theology and Lutheran theology and, above all, between Luther's theology and the doctrine of the Lutheran churches as expressed in their confessional writings. This doctrine is the primary reference point for the ecumenical dialogues. Still, it is appropriate here to concentrate on Luther's theology because of the anniversary commemoration of 31 October 1517.

STRUCTURE OF THIS CHAPTER

94. This chapter focuses on only four topics within Luther's theology: justification, eucharist, ministry, and Scripture and tradition. Because of their importance in the life of the church, and on account of the controversies they occasioned for centuries, they have been extensively

treated in the Catholic–Lutheran dialogues. The following presentation harvests the results of these dialogues.

95. The discussion of each topic proceeds in three steps. Luther's perspective on each of the four theological themes is presented first, followed by a short description of Catholic concerns regarding that topic. A summary then shows how Luther's theology has been brought into conversation with Catholic doctrine in ecumenical dialogue. This section highlights what has been jointly affirmed and identifies remaining differences.

96. An important topic for further discussion is how we can deepen our convergence on those issues where we still have different emphases, especially with respect to the doctrine of the church.

97. It is important to note that not all dialogue statements between Lutherans and Catholics carry the same weight of consensus, nor have they all been equally received by Catholics and Lutherans. The highest level of authority lies with the *Joint Declaration on the Doctrine of Justification*, signed by representatives of the Lutheran World Federation and the Roman Catholic Church in Augsburg, Germany, on 31 October 1999 and affirmed by the World Methodist Council in 2006. The sponsoring bodies have received other international and national dialogue commission reports, but these reports vary in their impact on the theology and life of Lutheran and Catholic communities. Church leaders now share the ongoing responsibility for appreciating and receiving the accomplishments of ecumenical dialogues.

Martin Luther's medieval heritage

98. Martin Luther was deeply embedded in the late Middle Ages. He could be all at once receptive to, critically distant from, or in the process of moving beyond its theologies. In 1505, he became a brother of the order of Augustinian hermits in Erfurt and, in 1512, a professor of sacred theology in Wittenberg. In this position, he focused his theological work primarily on the interpretation of biblical Scriptures. This emphasis on Holy Scripture was fully in line with what the rules of the order of the Augustinian Hermits expected a friar to do, namely to study and meditate on the Bible not only for his own personal benefit, but also for the spiritual benefit of others. The church fathers, especially Augustine, played a vital role in the development

and final shape of Luther's theology. "Our theology and St. Augustine are making progress,"[1] he wrote in 1517, and in the "Heidelberg Disputation" (1518) he refers to St Augustine as "the most faithful interpreter"[2] of the apostle Paul. Thus, Luther was very deeply rooted in the patristic tradition.

MONASTIC AND MYSTICAL THEOLOGY

99. While Luther had a predominantly critical attitude toward scholastic theologians, as an Augustinian hermit for twenty years, he lived, thought, and did theology in the tradition of monastic theology. One of the most influential monastic theologians was Bernard of Clairvaux, whom Luther highly appreciated. Luther's way of interpreting Scripture as the place of encounter between God and human beings shows clear parallels with Bernard's interpretation of Scripture.

100. Luther was also deeply rooted in the mystical tradition of the late medieval period. He found help in, and felt understood by, the German sermons of John Tauler (d. 1361). In addition, Luther himself published the mystical text, *Theologia deutsch* ("German Theology," 1518), which had been written by an unknown author. This text became widespread and well known through Luther's publication of it.

101. Throughout his whole life, Luther was very grateful to the superior of his order, John of Staupitz, and his Christ-centered theology, which consoled Luther in his afflictions. Staupitz was a representative of nuptial mysticism. Luther repeatedly acknowledged his helpful influence, saying, "Staupitz started this doctrine"[3] and praising him for "first of all being my father in this doctrine, and having given birth [to me] in Christ."[4] In the late Middle Ages, a theology was developed for the laity. This theology (*Frömmigkeitstheologie*) reflected upon the Christian life in practical terms and was oriented to the practice of piety. Luther was stimulated by this theology to write treatises of his own for the

1. Luther, "Letter to John Lang, Wittenberg, May 18, 1517," tr. Gottfried Krodel, in *LW* 48:44; WA *Briefwechsel* [*WAB*] 1; 99, 8.

2. Luther, 'Heidelberg Disputation," tr. Harold J. Grimm, in *LW* 31:39; WA 1; 353, 14.

3. *WA TR* 1; 245, 12.

4. Luther, "Letter to Elector John Frederick, March 25, 1545," quoted in Heiko Obermann, *Luther: Man between God and the Devil*, tr. Eileen Walliser-Schwarzbart (New Haven & London: Yale University Press, 1989), 152; *WAB* 11, 67, 7f.; *WAB* 11, 67, 7f.

laity. He took up many of the same topics but gave them his own distinct treatment.

JUSTIFICATION

LUTHER'S UNDERSTANDING OF JUSTIFICATION

102. Luther gained one of his basic Reformation insights from reflecting on the sacrament of penance, especially in relation to Matthew 16:18. In his late medieval education, he was trained to understand that God would forgive a person who was contrite for his or her sin by performing an act of loving God above all things, to which God would respond according to God's covenant (*pactum*) by granting anew God's grace and forgiveness (*facienti quod in se est deus non denegat gratiam*),[5] so that the priest could only declare that God had already forgiven the penitent's sin. Luther concluded that Matthew 16 said just the opposite, namely that the priest declared the penitent righteous, and by this act on behalf of God, the sinner actually became righteous.

Word of God as promise

103. Luther understood the words of God as words that create what they say and as having the character of promise (*promissio*). Such a word of promise is said in a particular place and time, by a particular person, and is directed to a particular person. A divine promise is directed toward a person's faith. Faith in turn grasps what is promised as promised to the believer personally. Luther insisted that such faith is the only appropriate response to a word of divine promise. A human being is called to look away from him- or herself and to look only at the word of God's promise and trust fully in it. Since faith grounds us in Christ's promise, it grants the believer full assurance of salvation. Not to trust in this word would make God a liar or one on whose word one could not ultimately rely. Thus, in Luther's view, unbelief is the greatest sin against God.

104. In addition to structuring the dynamic between God and the penitent

---

5. "God will not deny his grace to the one who is doing what is in him."

within the sacrament of penance, the relationship of promise and trust also shapes the relationship between God and human beings in the proclamation of the Word. God wishes to deal with human beings by giving them words of promise—sacraments are also such words of promise—that show God's saving will towards them. Human beings, on the other hand, should deal with God only by trusting in his promises. Faith is totally dependent on God's promises; it cannot create the object in which human beings put their trust.

105. Nevertheless, trusting God's promise is not a matter of human decision; rather, the Holy Spirit reveals this promise as trustworthy and thus creates faith in a person. Divine promise and human belief in that promise belong together. Both aspects need to be stressed, the "objectivity" of the promise and the "subjectivity" of faith. According to Luther, God not only reveals divine realities as information with which the intellect must agree; God's revelation also always has a soteriological purpose directed towards the faith and salvation of believers who receive the promises that God gives "for you" as words of God "for me" or "for us" (*pro me, pro nobis*).

106. God's own initiative establishes a saving relation to the human being; thus salvation happens by grace. The gift of grace can only be received, and since this gift is mediated by a divine promise, it cannot be received except by faith, and not by works. Salvation takes place **by grace alone**. Nevertheless, Luther constantly emphasized that the justified person would do good works in the Spirit.

By Christ alone

107. God's love for human beings is centered, rooted, and embodied in Jesus Christ. Thus, "by grace alone" is always to be explained by "by Christ alone." Luther describes the relationship of human persons with Christ by using the image of a spiritual marriage. The soul is the bride; Christ is the bridegroom; faith is the wedding ring. According to the laws of marriage, the properties of the bridegroom (righteousness) become the properties of the bride, and the properties of the bride (sin) become the properties of the bridegroom. This "joyful exchange" is the forgiveness of sins and salvation.

108. The image shows that something external, namely Christ's righteousness, becomes something internal. It becomes the property of the soul,

but only in union with Christ through trust in his promises, not in separation from him. Luther insists that our righteousness is totally external because it is Christ's righteousness, but it has to become totally internal by faith in Christ. Only if both sides are equally emphasized is the reality of salvation properly understood. Luther states, "It is precisely in faith that Christ is present."[6] Christ is "for us" (*pro nobis*) and in us (*in nobis*), and we are in Christ (*in Christo*).

Significance of the law

109. Luther also perceived human reality, with respect to the law in its theological or spiritual meaning, from the perspective of what God requires from us. Jesus expresses God's will by saying, "You shall love the Lord your God with all your heart and with all your soul and with all your mind" (Mt 22:37). That means that God's commandments are fulfilled only by total dedication to God. This includes not only the will and the corresponding outward actions, but also all aspects of the human soul and heart such as emotions, longing, and human striving, that is, those aspects and movements of the soul either not under the control of the will or only indirectly and partially under the control of the will through the virtues.

110. In the legal and moral spheres, there exists an old rule, intuitively evident, that nobody can be obliged to do more than he or she is able to do (*ultra posse nemo obligatur*). Thus, in the Middle Ages, many theologians were convinced that this commandment to love God must be limited to the will. According to this understanding, the commandment to love God does not require that all motions of the soul should be directed and dedicated to God. Rather, it would be enough that the will loves (i.e., wills) God above all (*diligere deum super omnia*).

111. Luther argued, however, that there is a difference between a legal and a moral understanding of the law, on the one hand, and a theological understanding of it, on the other. God has not adapted God's commandments to the conditions of the fallen human being. Instead, theologically understood, the commandment to love God shows the situation and the misery of human beings. As Luther wrote in the "Disputation

6. WA 40/II; 229, 15.

against Scholastic Theology," "Spiritually that person [only] does not kill, does not do evil, does not become enraged when he neither becomes angry nor lusts."[7] In this respect, divine law is not primarily fulfilled by external actions or acts or the will but by the wholehearted dedication of the whole person to the will of God.

Participation in Christ's righteousness

112. Luther's position, that God requires wholehearted dedication in fulfilling God's law, explains why Luther emphasized so strongly that we totally depend on Christ's righteousness. Christ is the only person who totally fulfilled God's will, and all other human beings can only become righteous in a strict, i.e., theological sense, if we participate in Christ's righteousness. Thus, our righteousness is external insofar as it is Christ's righteousness, but it must become our righteousness, that is, internal, by faith in Christ's promise. Only by participation in Christ's wholehearted dedication to God can we become wholly righteous.

113. Since the gospel promises us, "Here is Christ and his Spirit," participation in Christ's righteousness is never realized without being under the power of the Holy Spirit who renews us. Thus, becoming righteous and being renewed are intimately and inseparably connected. Luther did not criticize fellow theologians such as Gabriel Biel for too strong an emphasis on the transforming power of grace; on the contrary, he objected that they did not emphasize it strongly enough as being fundamental to any real change in the believer.

Law and gospel

114. According to Luther, this renewal will never come to fulfillment as long as we live. Therefore, another model of explaining human salvation, taken from the Apostle Paul, became important for Luther. In Romans 4:3, Paul refers to Abraham in Genesis 15:6 ("Abraham believed God, and it was reckoned to him as righteousness") and concludes, "To one

---

7. Luther, "Disputation against Scholastic Theology (1517)," tr. Harold J. Grimm, *LW* 31:13; *WA* 1, 227, 17–18.

who without works trusts him who justifies the ungodly, such faith is reckoned as righteousness" (Rom 4:5).

115. This text from Romans incorporates the forensic imagery of someone in a courtroom being declared righteous. If God declares someone righteous, this changes his or her situation and creates a new reality. God's judgment does not remain "outside" the human being. Luther often uses this Pauline model in order to emphasize that the whole person is accepted by God and saved, even though the process of the inner renewal of the justified into a person wholly dedicated to God will not come to an end in this earthly life.

116. As believers who are in the process of being renewed by the Holy Spirit, we still do not completely fulfill the divine commandment to love God wholeheartedly and do not meet God's demand. Thus the law will accuse us and identify us as sinners. With respect to the law, theologically understood, we believe that we are still sinners. But, with respect to the gospel that promises us "Here is Christ's righteousness," we are righteous and justified since we believe in the gospel's promise. This is Luther's understanding of the Christian believer who is at the same time justified and yet a sinner (*simul iustus et peccator*).

117. This is no contradiction since we must distinguish two relations of the believer to the Word of God: the relation to the Word of God as the law of God insofar as it judges the sinner, and the relation to the Word of God as the gospel of God insofar as Christ redeems. With respect to the first relation we are sinners; with respect to the second relation we are righteous and justified. This latter is the predominant relationship. That means that Christ involves us in a process of continuous renewal as we trust in his promise that we are eternally saved.

118. This is why Luther emphasized the freedom of a Christian so strongly: the freedom of being accepted by God by grace alone and by faith alone in Christ's promises, the freedom from the accusation of the law by the forgiveness of sins, and the freedom to serve one's neighbor spontaneously without seeking merits in doing so. The justified person is, of course, obligated to fulfill God's commandments, and will do so under the motivation of the Holy Spirit. As Luther declared in the Small Catechism: "We are to fear and love God, so that we . . . ," after which follow his explanations of the Ten Commandments.[8]

---

8. Luther, "The Small Catechism," in *BC*, 351–54.

CATHOLIC CONCERNS REGARDING JUSTIFICATION

119. Even in the sixteenth century, there was a significant convergence between Lutheran and Catholic positions concerning the need for God's
mercy and humans' inability to attain salvation by their own efforts.
The Council of Trent clearly taught that the sinner cannot be justified
either by the law or by human effort, anathematizing anyone who said
that "man can be justified before God by his own works which are done
either by his own natural powers, or through the teaching of the Law,
and without divine grace through Christ Jesus."[9]

120. Catholics, however, had found some of Luther's positions troubling.
Some of Luther's language caused Catholics to worry whether he denied personal responsibility for one's actions. This explains why the
Council of Trent emphasized the human person's responsibility and
capacity to cooperate with God's grace. Catholics stressed that the justified should be involved in the unfolding of grace in their lives. Thus,
for the justified, human efforts contribute to a more intense growth in
grace and communion with God.

121. Furthermore, according to the Catholic reading, Luther's doctrine of
"forensic imputation" seemed to deny the creative power of God's grace
to overcome sin and transform the justified. Catholics wished to emphasize not only the forgiveness of sins but also the sanctification of
the sinner. Thus, in sanctification the Christian receives that "justice
of God" whereby God makes us just.

LUTHERAN–ROMAN CATHOLIC DIALOGUE ON JUSTIFICATION

122. Luther and the other reformers understood the doctrine of the justification of sinners as the "first and chief article,"[10] the "guide and judge
over all parts of Christian doctrine."[11] That is why a division on this
point was so grave and the work to overcome this division became a
matter of highest priority for Catholic-Lutheran relations. In the second half of the twentieth century, this controversy was the subject of
extensive investigations by individual theologians and a number of
national and international dialogues.

9. Council of Trent, Sixth Session, 13 January 1547, can. 1
10. Luther, "Smalcald Articles," in *BC*, 301.
11. *WA* 39/1, 2–3, 205.

123. The results of these investigations and dialogues are summarized in the *Joint Declaration on the Doctrine of Justification* and were, in 1999, officially received by the Roman Catholic Church and the Lutheran World Federation. The following account is based on this Declaration, which offers a differentiating consensus comprised of common statements along with different emphases of each side, with the claim that these differences do not invalidate the commonalities. It is thus a consensus that does not eliminate differences, but rather explicitly includes them.

By grace alone

124. Together Catholics and Lutherans confess: "By grace alone, in faith in Christ's saving work and not because of any merit on our part, we are accepted by God and receive the Holy Spirit, who renews our hearts while equipping and calling us to good works" (*JDDJ* 15). The phrase "by grace alone" is further explained in this way: "the message of justification . . . tells us that as sinners our new life is solely due to the forgiving and renewing mercy that God imparts as a gift and we receive in faith, and never can merit in any way" (*JDDJ* 17).[12]

125. It is within this framework that the limits and the dignity of human freedom can be identified. The phrase "by grace alone," in regard to a human being's movement toward salvation, is interpreted in this way: "We confess together that all persons depend completely on the saving grace of God for their salvation. The freedom they possess in relation to persons and the things of this world is no freedom in relation to salvation" (*JDDJ* 19).

126. When Lutherans insist that a person can only receive justification, they mean, however, thereby "to exclude any possibility of contributing to one's own justification, but do not deny that believers are fully involved personally in their faith, which is effected by God's Word" (*JDDJ* 21).

127. When Catholics speak of preparation for grace in terms of "cooperation," they mean thereby a "personal consent" of the human being that is "itself an effect of grace, not an action arising from innate human abilities" (*JDDJ* 20). Thus, they do not invalidate the common expres-

---

12. The Lutheran World Federation and the Roman Catholic Church, *Joint Declaration on the Doctrine of Justification* (Grand Rapids, MI, Cambridge: Eerdmans, 2000) [= *JDDJ*].

sion that sinners are "incapable of turning by themselves to God to seek deliverance, of meriting their justification before God, or of attaining salvation by their own abilities. Justification takes place solely by God's grace" (*JDDJ* 19).

128. Since faith is understood not only as affirmative knowledge, but also as the trust of the heart that bases itself on the Word of God, it can further be said jointly: "Justification takes place 'by grace alone' (*JD* nos 15 and 16), by faith alone; the person is justified 'apart from works' (Rom 3:28, cf. *JD* no. 25)" (*JDDJ*, Annex 2C).[13]

129. What was often torn apart and attributed to one or the other confession but not to both is now understood in an organic coherence: "When persons come by faith to share in Christ, God no longer imputes to them their sin and through the Holy Spirit effects in them an active love. These two aspects of God's gracious action are not to be separated" (*JDDJ* 22).

Faith and good works

130. It is important that Lutherans and Catholics have a common view of how the coherence of faith and works is seen: believers "place their trust in God's gracious promise by justifying faith, which includes hope in God and love for him. Such a faith is active in love and thus the Christian cannot and should not remain without works" (*JDDJ* 25). Therefore, Lutherans also confess the creative power of God's grace which "affects all dimensions of the person and leads to a life in hope and love" (*JDDJ* 26). "Justification by faith alone" and "renewal" must be distinguished but not separated.

131. At the same time, "whatever in the justified precedes or follows the free gift of faith is neither the basis of justification nor merits it" (*JDDJ* 25). That is why the creative effect Catholics attribute to justifying grace is not meant to be a quality without relation to God, or a "human possession to which one could appeal over against God" (*JDDJ* 27). Rather, this view takes into account that within the new relationship with God the righteous are transformed and made children of God who live in new communion with Christ: "This new

13. Ibid., Official Common Statement by the Lutheran World Federation and the Roman Catholic Church, 43ff.

personal relation to God is grounded totally on God's graciousness and remains constantly dependent on the salvific and creative working of the gracious God, who remains true to himself, so that one can rely upon him" (*JDDJ* 27).

132. To the question of good works, Catholics and Lutherans state together: "We also confess that God's commandments retain their validity for the justified" (*JDDJ* 31). Jesus himself, as well as the apostolic Scriptures, "admonish[es] Christians to bring forth the works of love" which "follow justification and are its fruits" (*JDDJ* 37). So that the binding claim of the commandments might not be misunderstood, it is said: "When Catholics emphasize that the righteous are bound to observe God's commandments, they do not thereby deny that through Jesus Christ God has mercifully promised to his children the grace of eternal life" (*JDDJ* 33).

133. Both Lutherans and Catholics can recognize the value of good works in view of a deepening of the communion with Christ (cf. *JDDJ* 38f.), even if Lutherans emphasize that righteousness, as acceptance by God and sharing in the righteousness of Christ, is always complete. The controversial concept of merit is explained thus: "When Catholics affirm the 'meritorious' character of good works, they wish to say that, according to the biblical witness, a reward in heaven is promised to these works. Their intention is to emphasize the responsibility of persons for their actions, not to contest the character of those works as gifts, or far less to deny that justification always remains the unmerited gift of grace" (*JDDJ* 38).

134. To the much discussed question of the cooperation of human beings, a quotation from the Lutheran Confessions is taken in the Appendix to the *Joint Declaration on the Doctrine of Justification* as a common position in the most remarkable way: "The working of God's grace does not exclude human action: God effects everything, the willing and the achievement, therefore, we are called to strive (cf. Phil 2:12ff.). 'As soon as the Holy Spirit has initiated his work of regeneration and renewal in us through the Word and the holy sacraments, it is certain that we can and must cooperate by the power of the Holy Spirit. . . .'"[14]

---

14. *JDDJ*, Annex 2C, quoting "The Formula of Concord, Solid Declaration," II. 64f., in *BC*, 556.

SIMUL IUSTUS ET PECCATOR

135. In the debate over the differences in saying that a Christian is "simultaneously justified and a sinner," it was shown that each side does not understand exactly the same thing by the words "sin," "concupiscence," and "righteousness." It is necessary to concentrate not only on the formulation but also on the content in order to arrive at a consensus. With Romans 6:12 and 2 Corinthians 5:17, Catholics and Lutherans say that, in Christians, sin must not and should not reign. They further declare with 1 John 1:8–10 that Christians are not without sin. They speak of the "contradiction to God within the selfish desires of the old Adam" also in the justified, which makes a "lifelong struggle" against it necessary (*JDDJ* 28).

136. This tendency does not correspond to "God's original design for humanity," and it is "objectively in contradiction to God" (*JDDJ* 30), as Catholics say. Because, for them, sin has the character of an act, Catholics do not speak here of sin, while Lutherans see in this God-contradicting tendency a refusal to give oneself wholly to God and therefore call it sin. But both emphasize that this God-contradicting tendency does not divide the justified from God.

137. Under the presuppositions of his own theological system and after studying Luther's writings, Cardinal Cajetan concluded, that Luther's understanding of the assurance of faith implied establishing a new church. Catholic-Lutheran dialogue has identified the different thought forms of Cajetan and Luther that led to their mutual misunderstanding. Today, it can be said: "Catholics can share the concern of the Reformers to ground faith in the objective reality of Christ's promise, to look away from one's own experience, and to trust in Christ's forgiving word alone (cf. Mt 16:19; 18:18)" (*JDDJ* 36).

138. Lutherans and Catholics have each condemned the other confession's teachings. Therefore, the differentiating consensus as represented in the *Joint Declaration on the Doctrine of Justification* contains a double aspect. On the one hand, the Declaration claims that the mutual rejections of Catholic and Lutheran teaching as depicted there do not apply to the other confession. On the other, the Declaration positively affirms a consensus in the basic truths of the doctrine of justification: "The understanding of the doctrine of justification set forth in this Declaration shows that a consensus in basic truths of the doctrine of justification exists between Lutherans and Catholics" (*JDDJ* 40).

139. "In light of this consensus the remaining differences of language, theological elaboration, and emphasis in the understanding of justification are acceptable. Therefore the Lutheran and the Catholic explications of justification are in their differences open to one another and do not destroy the consensus regarding the basic truths" (*JDDJ* 40). "Thus the doctrinal condemnations of the sixteenth century, in so far as they relate to the doctrine of justification, appear in a new light: The teaching of the Lutheran churches presented in this Declaration does not fall under the condemnations from the Council of Trent. The condemnations in the Lutheran Confessions do not apply to the teaching of the Roman Catholic Church presented in this Declaration" (*JDDJ* 41). This is a highly remarkable response to the conflicts over this doctrine that lasted for nearly half a millennium.

EUCHARIST

LUTHER'S UNDERSTANDING OF THE LORD'S SUPPER

140. For Lutherans as well as Catholics the Lord's Supper is a precious gift in which Christians find nourishment and consolation for themselves, and where the church is ever anew gathered and built up. Hence the controversies about the sacrament cause pain.

141. Luther understood the sacrament of the Lord's Supper as a *testamentum*, the promise of someone who is about to die, as is evident from the Latin version of the words of institution. At first, Luther perceived Christ's promise (*testamentum*) as promising grace and forgiveness of sins but, in the debate with Huldrych Zwingli, he emphasized his belief that Christ gives himself, his body and blood, that are really present. Faith does not make Christ present; it is Christ who gives himself, his body and blood, to communicants, whether or not they believe this. Thus, Luther's opposition to the contemporary doctrine was not that he denied the real presence of Jesus Christ, but rather concerned how to understand the "change" in the Lord's Supper.

Real presence of Christ

142. The Fourth Lateran Council (1215) used the verb *transubstantiare*, which implies a distinction between substance and accidents.[15] Although this was for Luther a possible explanation of what happens in the Lord's Supper, he could not see how this philosophical explanation could be binding for all Christians. In any case, Luther himself strongly emphasized the real presence of Christ in the sacrament.

143. Luther understood Christ's body and blood to be present "in, with, and under" the species of bread and wine. There is an exchange of properties (*communicatio idiomatum*) between Christ's body and blood and the bread and wine. This creates a sacramental union between bread and Christ's body, and the wine and Christ's blood. This new type of union, formed by the sharing of properties, is analogous to the union of the divine and human natures in Christ. Luther also compared this sacramental union to the union of iron and fire in a fiery iron.

144. As a consequence of his understanding of the words of institution ("Drink of it, all of you," Mt 26:27), Luther criticized the practice of forbidding lay people to receive communion under both species, bread and wine. He did not argue that lay people would then only receive half of Christ, but affirmed that they would indeed receive the whole or full Christ in either species. Luther, however, denied that the church was entitled to withdraw the species of the wine from the laity since the words of institution are very clear about this. Catholics remind Lutherans that pastoral reasons were the principal motivation for introducing the practice of communion under one species.

145. Luther understood the Lord's Supper also as a communal event, a real meal, where the blessed elements are meant to be consumed, not preserved, after the celebration. He urged the consumption of all the elements so that the question about the duration of Christ's presence would not come up at all.[16]

15. The Fourth Lateran General Council, Symbol of Lateran (1215), *DH* 802.

16. Luther had instructed the Lutheran pastor Simon Wolferinus not to mix leftover consecrated eucharistic elements with consecrated ones. Luther told him to "do what we do here [i.e., in Wittenberg], namely, to eat and drink the remains of the Sacrament with the communicants so that it is not necessary to raise the scandalous and dangerous questions about when the action of the Sacrament ends" (*Luthers Werke—Weimarer Ausgabe, Briefwechsel,* X: 348f.).

Eucharistic sacrifice

146. Luther's main objection to Catholic eucharistic doctrine was directed against an understanding of the Mass as a sacrifice. The theology of the eucharist as real remembrance (*anamnesis, Realgedächtnis*), in which the unique and once-for-all sufficient sacrifice of Christ (Heb 9:1–10:18) makes itself present for the participation of the faithful, was no longer fully understood in late medieval times. Thus, many took the celebration of the Mass to be another sacrifice in addition to the one sacrifice of Christ. According to a theory stemming from Duns Scotus, the multiplication of Masses was thought to effect a multiplication of grace and to apply this grace to individual persons. That is why at Luther's time, for example, thousands of private masses were said every year at the castle church of Wittenberg.

147. Luther insisted that, according to the words of institution, Christ gives himself in the Lord's Supper to those who receive him and that, as a gift, Christ could only be received in faith but not offered. If Christ were offered to God, the inner structure and direction of the eucharist would be inverted. In Luther's eyes, understanding the eucharist as sacrifice would mean that it was a good work that we perform and offer to God. But he argued that just as we cannot be baptized in place of someone else, we cannot participate in the eucharist on behalf of and for the benefit of someone else. Instead of receiving the most precious gift that Christ himself is and offers to us, we would be attempting to offer something to God, thereby transforming a divine gift into a good work.

148. Nevertheless, Luther could see a sacrificial element in the Mass, the sacrifice of thanksgiving and praise. It is indeed a sacrifice in that by giving thanks a person acknowledges that he or she is in need of the gift and that his or her situation will change only by receiving the gift. Thus, true receiving in faith contains an active dimension that is not to be underestimated.

CATHOLIC CONCERNS REGARDING THE EUCHARIST

149. On the Catholic side, Luther's rejection of the concept of "transubstantiation" raised doubts whether the doctrine of the real presence of Christ had been fully affirmed in his theology. Although the Council of Trent

admitted that we can hardly express with words the manner of his presence and distinguished the doctrine of the conversion of elements from its technical explanation, it however declared, "the holy Catholic Church has suitably and properly called this change transubstantiation."[17] This concept seemed, in the Catholic view, to be the best guarantee for maintaining the real presence of Jesus Christ in the species of bread and wine and for assuring that the full reality of Jesus Christ is present in each of the species. When Catholics insist on a transformation of the created elements themselves, they want to highlight God's creative power, which brings about the new creation in the midst of the old creation.

150. While the Council of Trent defended the practice of adoration of the Blessed Sacrament, it took as its starting point that the primary purpose of the eucharist is the communion of the faithful. The eucharist was instituted by Christ to be consumed as spiritual food.[18]

151. As a result of the loss of an integrative concept of commemoration, Catholics were faced with the difficulty of the lack of adequate categories with which to express the sacrificial character of the eucharist. Committed to a tradition going back to patristic times, Catholics did not want to abandon the identification of the eucharist as a real sacrifice even while they struggled to affirm the identity of this eucharistic sacrifice with the unique sacrifice of Christ. The renewal of sacramental and liturgical theology as articulated in the Second Vatican Council was needed to revitalize the concept of commemoration (*anamnesis*) (*SC* 47; *LG* 3).

152. In their ecumenical dialogue, Lutherans and Catholics could both benefit from insights of the liturgical movement and new theological insights. Through the retrieval of the notion of *anamnesis*, both have been led to a better understanding of how the sacrament of the eucharist as a memorial effectively makes present the events of salvation and, in particular, the sacrifice of Christ. Catholics could appreciate the many forms of Christ's presence within the liturgy of the eucharist, such as his presence in his word and in the assembly (*SC* 7). In light of the ineffability of the mystery of eucharist, Catholics have learned to reevaluate diverse expressions of faith in the real presence of Jesus Christ in the sacrament. Lutherans gained a new awareness of the reasons to deal respectfully with the blessed elements after the celebration.

17. Council of Trent, Thirteenth Session, 11 October 1551, Chapter IV.
18. Ibid., Chapter II.

153. The question of the reality of the presence of Jesus Christ in the Lord's Supper is not a matter of controversy between Catholics and Lutherans. The Lutheran–Roman Catholic dialogue on the eucharist was able to state: "The Lutheran tradition affirms the Catholic tradition that the consecrated elements do not simply remain bread and wine but rather by the power of the creative word are given as the body and blood of Christ. In this sense Lutherans also could occasionally speak, as does the Greek tradition, of a change" (*Eucharist* 51).[19] Both Catholics and Lutherans "have in common a rejection of a spatial or natural manner of presence, and a rejection of an understanding of the sacrament as only commemorative or figurative" (*Eucharist* 16).[20]

Common understanding of the real presence of Christ

154. Lutherans and Catholics can together affirm the real presence of Jesus Christ in the Lord's Supper: "In the Sacrament of the Lord's Supper Jesus Christ true God and true man, is present wholly and entirely, in his Body and Blood, under the signs of bread and wine" (*Eucharist* 16). This common statement affirms all the essential elements of faith in the eucharistic presence of Jesus Christ without adopting the conceptual terminology of transubstantiation. Thus Catholics and Lutherans understand that "the exalted Lord is present in the Lord's Supper in the body and blood he gave with his divinity and his humanity through the word of promise in the gifts of bread and wine in the power of the Holy Spirit for reception through the congregation."[21]

155. To the question of the real presence of Jesus Christ and its theological understanding is joined the question of the duration of this presence and with it the question of the adoration of Christ present in the sacrament also after the celebration. "Differences related to the duration of the eucharistic presence appear also in liturgical practice. Catholic and Lutheran Christians together confess that the eucharistic presence of the Lord Jesus Christ is directed toward believing reception, that it

19. Cf. "Apology of the Augsburg Confession" X, in *BC* 184–85.
20. Growth in Agreement I, 190–214.
21. Council of Trent, op. cit. (note 23), citing the Condemnations of the Reformation Era.

nevertheless is not confined only to the moment of reception, and that it does not depend on the faith of the receiver, however closely related to it this might be" (*Eucharist* 52).

156. The document *The Eucharist* requested that Lutherans deal respectfully with the eucharistic elements that are left over after the celebration of the Supper. At the same time, it cautioned Catholics to take care that the practice of eucharistic adoration "does not contradict the common conviction about the meal-character of the Eucharist" (*Eucharist* 55).[22]

Convergence in understanding eucharistic sacrifice

157. With regard to the issue that was of the greatest importance for the reformers, the eucharistic sacrifice, the Catholic–Lutheran dialogue stated as a basic principle: "Catholic and Lutheran Christians together recognize that in the Lord's Supper Jesus Christ 'is present as the Crucified who died for our sins and who rose again for our justification, as the once-for-all sacrifice for the sins of the world.' This sacrifice can be neither continued, nor repeated, nor replaced, nor complemented; but rather it can and should become ever effective anew in the midst of the congregation. There are different interpretations among us regarding the nature and extent of this effectiveness" (*Eucharist* 56).

158. The concept of *anamnesis* has helped to resolve the controversial question of how one sets the once-for-all sufficient sacrifice of Jesus Christ in right relationship to the Lord's Supper: "Through the remembrance in worship of God's saving acts, these acts themselves become present in the power of the Spirit, and the celebrating congregation is linked with the men and women who earlier experienced the saving acts themselves. This is the sense in which Christ's command at the Lord's Supper is meant: in the proclamation, in his own words, of his saving death, and in the repetition of his own acts at the Supper, the 'remembrance' comes into being in which Jesus' word and saving work themselves become present."[23]

22. The English translation confuses this sentence; refer to the German original, in H. Meyer, H. J. Urban and L. Vischer (eds), *Dokumente wachsender Übereinstimmung: Sämtliche Berichte und Konsenstexte interkonfessioneller Gespräche auf Weltebene 1931–1982* (Paderborn: Bonifatius and Frankfurt: Lembeck, 1983), 287.

23. *Condemnations of the Reformation Era*, 3.II.1.2, 86.

159. The decisive achievement was to overcome the separation of *sacrificium* (the sacrifice of Jesus Christ) from *sacramentum* (the sacrament). If Jesus Christ is really present in the Lord's Supper, then his life, suffering, death, and resurrection are also truly present together with his body, so that the Lord's Supper is "the true making present of the event on the cross."[24] Not only the effect of the event on the cross but also the event itself is present in the Lord's Supper without the meal being a repetition or completion of the cross event. The one event is present in a sacramental modality. The liturgical form of the holy meal must, however, exclude everything that could give the impression of repetition or completion of the sacrifice on the cross. If the understanding of the Lord's Supper as a real remembrance is consistently taken seriously, the differences in understanding the eucharistic sacrifice are tolerable for Catholics and Lutherans.

Communion in both kinds and the office of eucharistic ministry

160. Since the time of the Reformation, reception of the cup by the laity has been a characteristic practice of Lutheran worship services. Thus, for a long time this practice visibly distinguished the Lutheran Lord's Supper from the Catholic practice of offering communion to the laity only under the species of bread. Today the principle can be stated: "Catholics and Lutherans are at one in the conviction that bread and wine belong to the complete form of the Eucharist" (*Eucharist* 64). Nevertheless, differences remain in the practice of the Lord's Supper.

161. Since the question of the presidency of the eucharistic celebration is ecumenically of great importance, the necessity of a church-appointed minister is a significant commonality identified by the dialogue: "Catholic and Lutheran Christians are of the conviction that the celebration of the Eucharist involves the leadership of a minister appointed by the church" (*Eucharist* 65). Nevertheless, Catholics and Lutherans still understand the office of ministry differently.

24. Ibid., 3.II.1.4, 88.

Ministry

LUTHER'S UNDERSTANDING OF THE COMMON PRIESTHOOD
OF THE BAPTIZED AND ORDAINED OFFICE

162. In the New Testament, the word *hiereus* (priest; Latin, *sacerdos*) did not designate an office in the Christian congregation, even though Paul describes his apostolic ministry as that of a priest (Rom 15:16). Christ is the high priest. Luther understands the relationship of the believers to Christ as a "joyful exchange," in which the believer takes part in the properties of Christ, and thus also in his priesthood. "Now just as Christ by his birthright obtained these two prerogatives, so he imparts to them and shares them with everyone who believes in him according to the law of the above-mentioned marriage, according to which the wife owns whatever belongs to the husband. Hence all of us who believe in Christ are priests and kings in Christ, as 1 Peter 2[:9] says: 'You are a chosen race, God's own people, a royal priesthood, a priestly kingdom.'"[25] "[W]e are all consecrated priests through baptism."[26]

163. Even though in Luther's understanding all Christians are priests, he does not regard them all as ministers. "It is true that all Christians are priests, but not all are pastors. For to be a pastor one must be not only a Christian and a priest but must have an office and a field of work committed to him. This call and command make pastors and preachers."[27]

164. Luther's theological notion that all Christians are priests contradicted the ordering of society that had become widespread in the Middle Ages. According to Gratian, there were two types of Christians, clerics and the laity.[28] With his doctrine of the common priesthood, Luther intended to abolish the basis for this division. What a Christian is as a priest arises from participation in the priesthood of Christ. He or she brings the concerns of the people in prayer before God and the concerns of God to others through the transmission of the gospel.

165. Luther understood the office of the ordained to be a public service for the whole church. Pastors are *ministri* (servants). This office is not in competition with the common priesthood of all the baptized but,

25. Luther, "Freedom of a Christian," tr. W. A. Lambert, rev. Harold J. Grimm, in *LW* 31:354; *WA* 7; 27, 17–21.
26. Luther, "Christian Nobility," in *LW* 44:127; *WA* 6; 407, 22f.
27. Luther, "Psalm 82," tr. C. M. Jacobs, in *LW* 13:65; *WA* 31/1; 211, 17–20.
28. Gratian, *Decr.* 2.12.1.7.

rather, it serves them so that all Christian people can be priests to one another.

Divine institution of the ministry

166. For more than 150 years, one of the debates in Lutheran theology has been whether the ordained ministry depends on divine institution or human delegation. However, Luther speaks of "the office of pastor, which God has established, which must rule over the congregation with sermons and sacraments."[29] Luther sees this office rooted in Christ's suffering and death: "I hope, indeed, that believers, those who want to be called Christians, know very well that the spiritual estate has been established and instituted by God, not with gold or silver but with the precious blood and bitter death of his only Son, our Lord Jesus Christ [1 Pet 1:18–19]. From his wounds indeed flow the sacraments [. . .] He paid dearly that men might everywhere have this office of preaching, baptizing, loosing, binding, giving the sacrament, comforting, warning, and exhorting with God's word, and whatever else belongs to the pastoral office [. . .] The estate I am thinking of is rather one which has the office of preaching and the service of the word and sacraments and which imparts the Spirit and salvation."[30] Clearly, then, for Luther, God has established the office of minister.

167. No one, Luther believed, can establish himself in the office; one must be called to it. Starting in 1535, ordinations were performed in Wittenberg. They took place after an examination of the doctrine and life of the candidates and if there had been a call to a congregation. But the ordination was not carried out in the calling congregation but centrally in Wittenberg, since ordination was ordination to the service of the whole church.

168. The ordinations were performed with prayer and the laying on of hands. As the introductory prayer—that God would send workers to harvest the crop (Mt 9:38)—and the prayer for the Holy Spirit both made clear, God is the one who in reality is active in the ordination. In

---

29. Luther, "To the Christian Nobility," tr. C. M. Jacobs, rev. J. Atkinson, in *LW* 44, *WA* 6; 441, 24f.

30. Luther, "A Sermon on Keeping Children in School," tr. Charles M. Jacobs, rev. Robert C. Schulz, in *LW* 46:219–20; *WA* 30/2; 526, 34; 527, 14–21; 528, 18f., 25–27.

ordination, the call of God embraces the whole person. With trust that the prayer will be answered by God, the charge to go forth took place with the words of 1 Peter 5:2–4.[31] In one of the ordination formulas it says: "The office of the church is for all churches a very great and important thing and it is given and maintained by God alone."[32]

169. Because Luther's definition of a sacrament was stricter than was common during the Middle Ages, and because he perceived the Catholic sacrament of holy orders as chiefly serving the practice of the sacrifice of the Mass, he ceased to view ordination as a sacrament. Melanchthon, however, stated in the Apology to the Augsburg Confession: "But if ordination is understood with reference to the ministry of the Word, we have no objection to calling ordination a sacrament. For the ministry of the Word has the command of God and has magnificent promises like Romans 1[:16]: the gospel 'is the power of God for salvation to everyone who has faith.' Likewise, Isaiah 55[:11], '. . . so shall my word be that goes out from my mouth; it shall not return to me empty, but it shall accomplish that which I purpose. . . .' If ordination is understood in this way, we will not object to calling the laying on of hands as a sacrament. For the church has the mandate to appoint ministers, which ought to please us greatly because we know that God approves this ministry and is present in it."[33]

Office of the bishop

170. Because the bishops refused to ordain candidates who were sympathetic to the Reformation, the reformers practiced ordination by presbyters (pastors). In Article 28, the Augsburg Confession complains about the bishops' refusal to ordain. This forced the reformers to choose between retaining ordination by bishops or being faithful to what they understood to be the truth of the gospel.

171. The reformers were able to practice presbyteral ordination because they had learned from Peter Lombard's *Sentences* that the canons of the church recognized only two sacramental orders among the major orders, the diaconate and the presbyterate, and that, according to the

31. See the Wittenberger Ordinationszeugnisse, in WA *Briefwechsel* 12, 447–85.
32. *WA* 38 423, 21–25.
33. Apology XIII, "On the Number and Use of the Sacraments" 7, in *BC*, 220.

widespread understanding of the Middle Ages, the consecration of bishops imparted no sacramental character of its own.[34] The reformers explicitly referred to a letter by Jerome, who was convinced that, according to the New Testament, the offices of presbyter and bishop were the same with the exception that the bishop had the right to ordain. As the reformers noted, this letter to Evangelus had been received into the *Decretum Gratiani*.[35]

172. Luther and the reformers emphasized that there is only one ordained ministry, an office of the public proclamation of the gospel and administration of the sacraments, which are by their very nature public events. Nevertheless, from the beginning there was a differentiation in the office. From the first visitations, the office of superintendent developed, which had the special task of oversight over the pastors. Philip Melanchthon wrote in 1535: "Because in the church rulers are necessary, who will examine and ordain those who are called to ecclesial office, church law observes and exercises oversight upon the teaching of the priests. And if there were no bishops, one would nevertheless have to create them."[36]

CATHOLIC CONCERNS REGARDING THE COMMON PRIESTHOOD AND ORDINATION

173. The dignity and responsibility of all the baptized in and for the life of the church were not adequately emphasized in the late medieval period. Not until the Second Vatican Council did the magisterium present a theology of the church as the people of God and affirm the "true equality of all with regard to the dignity and action common to all the faithful concerning the building up of the body of Christ" (*LG* 32).

174. Within this framework, the Council developed the notion of the priesthood of the baptized and addressed its relationship to the ministerial

---

34. Peter Lombard, *Sent.* IV, dist. 24, cap. 12.

35. Philipp Melanchthon quoted Jerome's letter in his "De potestate et primatu papae tractatus," in *BC*, 340. See also *WA* 2; 230, 17–19; Jerome, "Letter 146 to Evangelus," in J.-P. Migne (ed.), *Patrologia Latina* XXII (Paris, 1845), 1192–95; "Decretum Gratiani," pars 1, dist. 93, in E. Friedberg (ed.), *Corpus Iuris Canonici* (Graz, 1955), 327–29.

36. Melanchthon, "Consilium de moderandis controversiis religionis," in C. G. Bretschneider (ed.), *Corpus Reformatorum*, vol. II (Halle: C. A. Schwetschke, 1895), 745f.; 1535).

priesthood. In Catholic theology, the ordained minister is sacramentally empowered to act in the name of Christ as well as in the name of the church.

175. Catholic theology is convinced that the office of bishop makes an indispensable contribution to the unity of the church. Catholics raise the question of how, without the episcopal office, church unity can be maintained in times of conflict. They have also been concerned that Luther's particular doctrine of the common priesthood did not adequately maintain the church's hierarchical structures, which are seen as divinely instituted.

LUTHERAN–ROMAN CATHOLIC DIALOGUE ON MINISTRY

176. Catholic-Lutheran dialogue has identified numerous commonalities as well as differences in the theology and institutional form of ordained offices, among them the ordination of women, now practiced by many Lutheran churches. One of the remaining questions is whether the Catholic Church can recognize the ministry of the Lutheran churches. Together Lutherans and Catholics can work out the relationship between the responsibility for the proclamation of the Word and the administration of the sacraments and the office of those ordained for this work. Together they can develop the distinctions among such tasks as *episkopé* and local and more regional offices.

Common understandings of the ministry

Priesthood of the baptized

177. The question arises of how the specificity of the tasks of the ordained are rightly set in relationship with the universal priesthood of all baptized believers. The study document *The Apostolicity of the Church* states, "Catholics and Lutherans are in agreement that all the baptized who believe in Christ share in the priesthood of Christ and are thus commissioned to 'proclaim the mighty acts of him who called you out of darkness into his marvelous light' (1 Pet 2:9). Hence no member lacks a part to play in the mission of the whole body" (*ApC* 273).

Divine source of the ministry

178. In understanding the ordained office, there is a common conviction about its divine source: "Catholics and Lutherans affirm together that God instituted the ministry and that it is necessary for the being of the church, since the word of God and its public proclamation in word and sacrament are necessary for faith in Jesus Christ to arise and be preserved and together with this for the church to come into being and be preserved as believers who make up the body of Christ in the unity of faith" (*ApC* 276).

Ministry of Word and sacrament

179. *The Apostolicity of the Church* identifies the fundamental task of ordained ministers for both Lutherans and Catholics as the proclamation of the gospel: "Ordained ministers have a special task within the mission of the church as a whole" (*ApC* 274). For both Catholics and Lutherans "the fundamental duty and intention of ordained ministry is public service of the word of God, the gospel of Jesus Christ, which the Triune God has commissioned the church to proclaim to all the world. Every office and every office-holder must be measured against this obligation" (*ApC* 274).

180. This emphasis on the ministerial task of proclaiming the gospel is common to Catholics and Lutherans (cf. *ApC* 247, 255, 257, 274). Catholics locate the origin of priestly ministry in the proclamation of the gospel. The Decree on Priests (*Presbyterorum Ordinis*) states, "The people of God is formed into one in the first place by the word of the living God, which is quite rightly expected from the mouth of priests. For since nobody can be saved who has not first believed, it is the first task of priests as co-workers of the bishops to preach the gospel of God to all" (*PO* 4, cited in *ApC* 247). "Catholics also declare that it is the task of ordained ministers to gather the people of God together by the word of God and to proclaim this to all so that they may believe" (*ApC* 274). Similarly, the Lutheran understanding is that "the ministry has its basis and criterion in the task of communicating the gospel to the **whole** congregation in such a compelling way that assurance of faith is awakened and made possible" (*ApC* 255).

181. Lutherans and Catholics also agree on the responsibility of ordained

leadership for the administration of the sacraments. Lutherans say, "The gospel bestows on those who preside over the churches the commission to proclaim the gospel, forgive sins, and administer the sacraments" (*ApC* 274).[37] Catholics also declare that priests are commissioned to administer the sacraments, which they consider to be "bound up with the Eucharist" and directed toward it as "the source and summit of all the preaching of the Gospel" (*PO* 5, cited in *ApC* 274).

182. *The Apostolicity of the Church* further comments, "It is worth noting the similarity between the descriptions of the ministerial functions of presbyters and of bishops. The same pattern of the threefold office—preaching, liturgy, leadership—is used for bishops and presbyters, and in the concrete life of the church precisely the latter carry out the ordinary exercise of these functions through which the church is built up, while the bishops have oversight over teaching and care for the communion among local communities. However the presbyters exercise their ministry in subordination to the bishops and in communion with them" (*ApC* 248).

Ordination rite

183. With respect to induction into this special office, there exists the following commonality: "Induction into this ministry takes place by ordination, in which a Christian is called and commissioned, by prayer and the laying on of hands, for the ministry of public preaching of the gospel in word and sacrament. That prayer is a plea for the Holy Spirit and the Spirit's gifts, made in the certainty that it will be heard" (*ApC* 277).

Local and regional ministry

184. Lutherans and Catholics can say together that the differentiation of the office "into a more local and a more regional office arises of necessity out of the intention and task of the ministry to be a ministry of

---

37. Citing Melanchthon, Treatise on the Power and Primacy of the Pope, *BC*, 340: *BSLK*, 489, 30–35.

unity in faith" (*ApC* 279). In Lutheran churches, the task of *episkopé* is perceived in various forms. Those who exercise supra-congregational ministry are designated in some places by titles other than "bishop," such as, ephorus, church president, superintendent, or synodal pastor. Lutherans understand that the ministry of *episkopé* is also exercised not only individually but also in such other forms, as synods, in which both ordained and non-ordained members participate together.[38]

Apostolicity

185. Even though Catholics and Lutherans perceive their ministerial structures to transmit the apostolicity of the church differently, they agree, "fidelity to the apostolic gospel has priority in the interplay of *traditio, successio* and *communio*" (*ApC* 291). They both agree, "the church is apostolic on the basis of fidelity to the apostolic gospel" (*ApC* 292). This agreement has consequences for Roman Catholic recognition that individuals "who exercise the office of supervision which in the Roman Catholic Church is performed by bishops" also "bear a special responsibility for the apostolicity of doctrine in their churches" and therefore cannot be excluded from "the circle of those whose consensus is according to the Catholic view the sign of apostolicity of doctrine" (*ApC* 291).

Service to the church universal

186. Lutherans and Catholics agree that the ministry serves the church universal. Lutherans "presuppose that the congregation assembled for worship stands in an essential relation to the universal church" and that this relation is intrinsic to the worshipping congregation, not something added to it (*ApC* 285). Even though Roman Catholic bishops "exercise their pastoral government over the portion of the People of God committed to their care, and not over other churches nor over

---

38. In 2007, the LWF Council adopted "Episcopal Ministry within the Apostolicity of the Church: The Lund Statement by the Lutheran World Federation—A Communion of Churches." While "not intended to be a magisterial document," the text seeks to clarify for the Lutheran Communion a number of questions concerning *episkopé*, with attention both to Lutheran tradition and to the fruits of ecumenical engagements. See https://ecumenism.net /archive/docu/2007_lwf_lund_episcopal_ministry_apostolicity_church_en.pdf.

the universal Church," each bishop is obliged to be "solicitous for the whole church" (*LG* 23). The Bishop of Rome by virtue of his office is "pastor of the whole Church" (*LG* 22).

Differences in understanding the ministry

The episcopacy

187. Significant differences with regard to the understanding of ministry in the church remain. *The Apostolicity of the Church* acknowledges that for Catholics the episcopate is the full form of ordained ministry and therefore the point of departure for the theological interpretation of church ministry. The document cites *Lumen Gentium* 21: "The holy synod teaches, moreover, that the fullness of the Sacrament of Orders is conferred by Episcopal consecration . . . [which] confers, together with the office of sanctifying, the offices also of teaching and ruling, which, however, of their very nature can be exercised only in hierarchical communion with the head and the members of the college" (cited in *ApC* 243).

188. The Second Vatican Council reaffirmed its understanding "that bishops have by divine institution taken the place of the apostles as pastors of the church in such wise that whoever hears them hears Christ and whoever rejects them rejects Christ and him who sent Christ" (*LG* 20). Nevertheless, it is Catholic doctrine "that an individual bishop is *not* in apostolic succession by his being part of a historically verifiable and uninterrupted chain of imposition of hands through his predecessors to one of the apostles," but instead that he is "in communion with the whole order of bishops which as a whole succeeds the apostolic college and its mission" (*ApC* 291).

189. This perspective on ministry, which begins with the episcopacy, represents a shift from the Council of Trent's focus on the priesthood and underlines the importance of the theme of apostolic succession, even though *Lumen Gentium* stressed the ministerial aspect of this succession without denying the doctrinal, missionary, and existential dimensions of apostolic succession (*ApC* 240). For this reason, Catholics identify the local church with the diocese, considering the essential elements of the church to be word, sacrament, and apostolic ministry in the person of the bishop (*ApC* 284).

Priesthood

190. Catholics differ from Lutherans in their interpretation of the sacramental identity of a priest and the relationship of the sacramental priesthood to the priesthood of Christ. They affirm that priests are "made sharers in a special way in Christ's priesthood and, by carrying out sacred functions, act as ministers of him who through his Spirit continually exercises his priestly role for our benefit in the liturgy" (*PO* 5).

Fullness of sacramental sign

191. For Catholics, Lutheran ordinations lack a fullness of sacramental sign. In Catholic doctrine, "the practice and doctrine of apostolic succession in the episcopate is, together with the threefold ministry, part of the complete structure of the church. This succession is realized in a corporate manner as bishops are taken into the college of Catholic bishops and thereby have the power to ordain. Therefore it is also Catholic doctrine that in Lutheran churches the sacramental sign of ordination is not fully present because those who ordain do not act in communion with the Catholic episcopal college. Therefore the Second Vatican Council speaks of a *defectus sacramenti ordinis* (*UR* 22) in these churches" (*ApC* 283).[39]

Worldwide ministry

192. Finally, Catholics and Lutherans differ in both the offices and authority of ministry and leadership beyond the regional level. For Catholics, the Roman Pontiff has "full, supreme, and universal power over the church" (*LG* 22). The college of bishops also exercises supreme and full power over the universal church "together with its head the Roman Pontiff, and never without this head" (*LG* 22). *The Apostolicity of the Church* notes various views among Lutherans regarding "the compe-

---

39. See Randall Lee and Jeffrey Gros, FSC (eds), *The Church as Koinonia of Salvation: Its Structures and Ministries* (Washington, D.C.: United States Conference of Catholic Bishops, 2005), 49–50, §§107–109.

tency of leadership bodies above the level of the individual churches and the binding force of their decisions" (*ApC* 287).

Considerations

193. In dialogue it has often been noted that the relationship of bishops and presbyters at the beginning of the sixteenth century was not understood as it was later by the Second Vatican Council. Presbyteral ordination at the time of the Reformation should therefore be considered with reference to the conditions of that period. It is also significant that the tasks of Catholic and Lutheran officeholders have broadly corresponded to one another.

194. In the course of history, the Lutheran ministerial office has been able to fulfill its task of keeping the church in the truth so that nearly five hundred years after the beginning of the Reformation it was possible to declare a Catholic-Lutheran consensus on the basic truths of the doctrine of justification. If, according to the judgment of the Second Vatican Council, the Holy Spirit uses "ecclesial communities" as means of salvation, it could seem that this work of the Spirit would have implications for some mutual recognition of ministry. Thus, the office of ministry presents both considerable obstacles to common understanding and also hopeful perspectives for rapprochement.[40]

SCRIPTURE AND TRADITION

LUTHER'S UNDERSTANDING OF SCRIPTURE, ITS INTERPRETATION, AND HUMAN TRADITIONS

195. The controversy that broke out in connection with the spread of Luther's Ninety-five Theses on indulgences very quickly raised the question of which authorities one can call upon at a time of struggle. The papal court theologian Sylvester Prierias argued in his first answer to

---

40. These questions have also been explored by the Ökumenischer Arbeitskreis evangelischer und katholischer Theologen; their work has been collected in *Das kirchliche Amt in apostolischer Nachfolge,* 3 vols (Freiburg: Herder and Göttingen: Vandenhoeck & Ruprecht, 2004, 2006, 2008).

Luther's theses on indulgences: "Whoever does not hold to the teaching of the Roman church and the pope as an infallible rule of faith from which the Holy Scripture also derives its power and authority: he is a heretic."[41] And John Eck replied to Luther: "The Scripture is not authentic without the authority of the church."[42] The conflict very quickly went from being a controversy about doctrinal questions (the right understanding of indulgences, penance, and absolution) to a question of authority in the church. In cases of conflict between different authorities, Luther could regard only Scripture as the ultimate judge because it had shown itself to be an efficacious and powerful authority, while other authorities merely drew their power from it.

196. Luther regarded Scripture as the first principle (*primum principium*)[43] on which all theological statements must directly or indirectly be grounded. As a professor, preacher, counselor, and conversation partner, he practiced theology as a consistent and complex interpretation of Scripture. He was convinced that Christians and theologians should not only adhere to Scripture but live and remain in it. He called it "the matrix of God in which he conceives us, bears us and gives us birth."[44]

197. The right way to study theology is, according to Luther, a three-step process of *oratio* [prayer], *meditatio* [meditation], *tentatio* [affliction or testing].[45] Asking the Holy Spirit to be the teacher, one should read Scripture in the presence of God, in prayer, and while meditating on the words of the Bible, be attentive to the situations in life that often seem to contradict what is found there. Through this process, Scripture proves its authority by overcoming those afflictions. As Luther said, "Note that the strength of the Scripture is this, that it is not changed into the one who studies it, but that it transforms one who loves it into itself and its strength."[46] In this experiential context it becomes obvious

41. Sylvester Prierias, "Dialogue de potestate papae," in P. Fabischand, E. Iserloh (eds), *Dokumente zur Causa Lutheri (1517–1521)*, vol. I (Münster: Aschendorff, 1988), 55.

42. John Eck, "Enchiridion locorum communium adversus Lutherum et alios hostes ecclesiae (1525–1543)," in P. Fraenkel (ed.), *Corpus Catholicorum* 34 (Münster: Ascendorff, 1979), 27.

43. See *WA* 7; 97, 16–98, 16.

44. *WA* 10/1, 1; 232, 13–14.

45. Luther, "Preface to the Wittenberg edition of Luther's German writings (1539)," tr. Robert R. Heitner, in *LW* 34:285; *WA* 50; 559, 5–660, 16.

46. Luther, "First Lectures on the Psalms," tr. Herbert J. A. Bouman, in *LW* 10:332; *WA* 3; 397, 9–11.

that a person not only interprets Scripture but is also interpreted by it, and this is what proves its power and authority.

198. Scripture is the witness to God's revelation; thus a theologian should carefully follow the way in which God's revelation is expressed in the biblical books (*modus loquendi scripturae*). Otherwise, God's revelation would not be taken fully into account. The manifold voices of Scripture are integrated into a whole by their reference to Jesus Christ: "Take Christ out of the Scriptures, and what else will you find in them?"[47] Thus "what inculcates Christ" (*was Christum treibet*) is the standard in addressing the problem of the canonicity and the limits of the canon. It is a standard developed from Scripture itself and in a few cases applied critically to particular books, like the letter of James.

199. Luther himself only rarely used the expression "*sola scriptura.*" His chief concern was that nothing could claim a higher authority than Scripture, and he turned with the greatest severity against anyone and anything that altered or displaced the statements of Scripture. But even when he asserted the authority of Scripture alone, he did not read Scripture alone but with reference to particular contexts and in relation to the Christological and trinitarian confessions of the early church, which for him expressed the intention and meaning of Scripture. He continued to learn Scripture through the Small and Large Catechisms, which he regarded as short summaries of Scripture, and practiced his interpretation with reference to the church fathers, especially Augustine. He also made intensive use of other earlier interpretations and drew on all the available tools of humanist philology. He carried out his interpretation of the Scripture in direct debate with the theological conceptions of his time and those of earlier generations. His reading of the Bible was experience-based and practiced consistently within the community of believers.

200. According to Luther, Holy Scripture does not oppose all tradition but only so-called human traditions. Of them he says, "We censure the doctrines of men not because men have spoken them, but because they are lies and blasphemies against the Scriptures. And the Scriptures, although they too are written by men, are neither of men nor from men but from God."[48] When evaluating another authority, the decisive

---

47. Luther, "Bondage of the Will," tr. Philip S. Watson with Benjamin Drewery, in *LW* 33:26; *WA* 18; 606, 29.

48. *WA* 10/2; 92, 4–7.

question for Luther was whether this authority obscures Scripture or brings home its message and so makes it meaningful in a particular context. Due to its external clarity, Scripture's meaning can be identified; due to the power of the Holy Spirit, Scripture can convince the human heart of its truth, the inner clarity of Scripture. In this sense, Scripture is its own interpreter.

CATHOLIC CONCERNS REGARDING SCRIPTURE, TRADITIONS, AND AUTHORITY

201. At a time when new questions concerning the discernment of traditions and the authority to interpret the Scripture arose, the Council of Trent as well as theologians of the time tried to give a balanced answer. The Catholic experience was that ecclesial life is enriched and determined by diverse factors not reducible to Scripture alone. Trent held up Scripture and non-written apostolic traditions as two means of handing on the gospel. This requires distinguishing apostolic traditions from church traditions, which are valuable, but secondary and alterable. Catholics were also concerned about the potential danger of doctrinal conclusions drawn from private interpretations of Scripture. In light of this, the Council of Trent asserted that scriptural interpretation was to be guided by the teaching authority of the church.

202. Catholic teachers like Melchior Cano developed the insight that assessing the authority of church teaching is complex. Cano developed a system of ten loci, or sources of theology, treating successively the authority of Scripture, oral tradition, the Catholic Church, the councils, the church fathers, the scholastic theologians, the value of nature, reason as manifested in science, the authority of philosophers, and the authority of history. Finally, he examines the use and application of these loci, or sources, in scholastic debate or theological polemics.[49]

203. During the following centuries, however, there was a tendency to isolate the magisterium as a binding interpretative authority from other theological loci. Ecclesiastical traditions were at times confused with apostolic traditions and thereby treated as equivalent material sources for the Christian faith. There was also a reluctance to recognize the

---

49. Melchior Cano, *De locis theologis*, Book 1, chap. 3 (Migne, *Theologiae cursus computus1* [Paris, 1837]), col. 82.

possibility of criticizing ecclesiastical traditions. The theology of Vatican II, on the whole, has a more balanced view of different authorities in the church and the relationship between Scripture and tradition. In *DV* 10, a magisterial text affirms for the first time that the teaching office of the church is "not above the Word of God but stands at its service."

204. The role of the Holy Scripture in the life of the church is strongly emphasized when the Second Vatican Council says, "the force and power in the word of God is so great that it stands as the support and energy of the Church, the strength of faith for her sons, the food of the soul, the pure and everlasting source of spiritual life" (*DV* 21).[50] Therefore, the faithful are admonished to practice the reading of the Scripture, in which God speaks to them, accompanied by prayer (*DV* 25).

205. Ecumenical dialogue helps Lutherans and Catholics arrive at a more differentiated view of the distinct points of reference and authorities which play a role in the process of realizing what the Christian faith means and how it should shape the life of the church.

THE CATHOLIC-LUTHERAN DIALOGUE
ON SCRIPTURE AND TRADITION

206. As a consequence of the biblical renewal that inspired the Dogmatic Constitution *Dei Verbum* of the Second Vatican Council, a new ecumenical understanding of the role and significance of the Holy Scripture has become possible. As the ecumenical document *Apostolicity of the Church* states, "Catholic doctrine, thus, does not hold what Reformation theology fears and wants at all costs to avoid, namely, a derivation of scriptural authority as canonical and binding from the authority of the church's hierarchy which makes known the canon" (*ApC* 400).

207. In dialogue, Catholics have emphasized convictions held in common with the Reformation, such as the efficacy of the Spirit-inspired biblical text "in conveying revealed truth that forms minds and hearts, as affirmed in 2 Tim. 3:17 and stated by Vatican II (*DV* 21–25)" (*ApC* 409). Catholics add, "this efficacy has been operative in the church over

50. www.vatican.va/archive/hist_councils/ii_vatican_council/documents/vat-ii_const _19651118_dei-verbum_en.html.

time, not only in individual believers but as well in the ecclesial tradition, both in high-level doctrinal expressions such as the rule of faith, creeds, and conciliar teaching, and in the principal structures of public worship . . . Scripture has made itself present in the tradition, which is therefore able to play an essential hermeneutical role. Vatican II does not say that the tradition gives rise to new truths beyond Scripture, but that it conveys certainty about revelation attested by Scripture" (*ApC* 410).

208. A fruit of ecumenical dialogue for Lutheran theology is its openness to the Catholic conviction that the efficacy of the Scripture is at work not only in individuals, but also in the church as a whole. Evidence for this lies in the role of the Lutheran Confessions in the Lutheran churches.

Scripture and tradition

209. Today, the role and significance of the Holy Scripture and tradition are therefore understood differently in the Roman Catholic Church than they were by Luther's theological opponents. Regarding the question of the authentic interpretation of Scripture, Catholics have explained, "When Catholic doctrine holds that the 'judgment of the church' has a role in authentic interpretation of Scripture, it does not attribute to the church's magisterium a monopoly over interpretation, which adherents of the Reformation rightly fear and reject. Before the Reformation, major figures had indicated the ecclesial plurality of interpreters. . . . When Vatican II speaks of the church having an 'ultimate judgment' (*DV* 12) it clearly eschews a monopolistic claim that the magisterium is the sole organ of interpretation, which is confirmed both by the century-old official promotion of Catholic biblical studies and the recognition in *DV* 12 of the role of exegesis in the maturing of magisterial teaching" (*ApC* 407).

210. Thus, Lutherans and Catholics are able jointly to conclude, "Therefore regarding Scripture and tradition, Lutherans and Catholics are in such an extensive agreement that their different emphases do not of themselves require maintaining the present division of the churches. In this area, there is unity in reconciled diversity" (*ApC* 448).[51]

---

51. These issues also have been explored in Germany by the Ökumenischer Arbeitskreis evangelischer und katholischer Theologen; their work is available in W. Pannenberg and Th.

LOOKING AHEAD: THE GOSPEL AND THE CHURCH

211. In addition to giving Catholics a better understanding of Martin Luther's theology, ecumenical dialogue, together with historical and theological research, gives both Lutherans and Catholics a better mutual understanding of each other's doctrines, their major points of agreement, and issues still needing ongoing conversation. The Church has been an important topic in these discussions.

212. The nature of the Church was a disputed topic at the time of the Reformation. The primary issue was the relationship between God's salvific action and the church, which both receives and communicates God's grace in Word and sacrament. The relationship between the gospel and the church was the theme of the first phase of the international Lutheran–Roman Catholic dialogue. Because of this Malta report, as well as many other subsequent ecumenical documents, it is possible today to understand better the Lutheran and the Catholic positions and to identify both the common understandings and the issues that require further consideration.

The church in the Lutheran tradition

213. In the Lutheran tradition, the church is understood as "the assembly of saints in which gospel is taught purely and the sacraments are administered rightly" (CA VII). This means that the spiritual life is centered in the local congregation gathered around pulpit and altar. This includes the dimension of the universal church since each individual congregation is connected to the others by pure preaching and right celebration of the sacraments, for which the ministry in the church is established. One should keep in mind that Luther in his Large Catechism called the church "the mother that begets and bears every Christian through the Word of God which the Holy Spirit reveals and proclaims. . . . The Holy Spirit will remain with the holy community [*Gemeine*] or Christian people until the Last Day. Through it he fetches us to Christ, using it to teach and preach the Word."[52]

Schneider (eds), *Verbindliches Zeugnis*, 3 vols (Freiburg: Herder and Göttingen: Vandenhoeck & Ruprecht, 1992, 1995, 1998).

52. Luther, "Large Catechism," in *BC*, 436–38 (translation altered); *BSLK* 665, 3–6; 667, 42–46.

The church in the Catholic tradition

214. The teaching of the Second Vatican Council in *Lumen Gentium* is essential to the Catholic understanding of the church. The council fathers explained the role of the church within salvation history in terms of sacramentality: "The church is in Christ like a sacrament or as a sign and instrument both of a very closely knit union with God and of the unity of the whole human race" (*LG* 1).

215. A basic concept for explaining this sacramental understanding of the church recurs in the notion of Mystery and affirms the inseparable relation between the visible and invisible aspects of the church. The council fathers taught: "Christ, the one Mediator, established and continually sustains here on earth His holy Church, the community of faith, hope and charity, as an entity with visible delineation through which He communicated truth and grace to all. But, the society structured with hierarchical organs and the Mystical Body of Christ, are not to be considered as two realities, nor are the visible assembly and the spiritual community, nor the earthly Church and the Church enriched with heavenly things; rather they form one complex reality which coalesces from a divine and a human element" (*LG* 8).

TOWARDS CONSENSUS

216. In the Lutheran–Roman Catholic conversations a clear consensus has emerged that the doctrine of justification and the doctrine of the church belong together. This common understanding is stated in the document *Church and Justification*: "Catholics and Lutherans together testify to the salvation that is bestowed only in Christ and by grace alone and is received in faith. They recite in common the creed, confessing 'one holy catholic and apostolic Church.' Both the justification of sinners and the Church are fundamental articles of faith" (*Church and Justification*, 4).

217. *Church and Justification* also states: "Strictly and properly speaking, we do not believe in justification and in the Church, but in the Father, who has mercy on us and who gathers us in the Church as his people; and in Christ who justifies us and whose body the Church is; and in the Holy Spirit who sanctifies us and dwells in the Church. Our faith encompasses justification and the Church as work of the triune God

which can be properly accepted only in faith in him" (*Church and Justification*, 5).

218. Although the documents *Church and Justification* and *Apostolicity of the Church* made significant contributions to a number of unresolved issues between Catholics and Lutherans, further ecumenical conversation is still needed on: the relation between the visibility and invisibility of the church, the relation between the universal and local church, the church as sacrament, the necessity of sacramental ordination in the life of the church, and the sacramental character of episcopal consecration. Future discussion must take into account the significant work already done in these and other important documents. This task is so urgent since Catholics and Lutherans have never ceased to confess together the faith in the "one, holy, catholic, and apostolic church."

CHAPTER V

Called to Common Commemoration

BAPTISM: THE BASIS FOR UNITY
AND COMMON COMMEMORATION

219. The church is the body of Christ. As there is only one Christ, so also he has only one body. Through baptism, human beings are made members of this body.

220. The Second Vatican Council teaches that people who are baptized and believe in Christ but do not belong to the Roman Catholic church "have been justified by faith in Baptism [and] are members of Christ's body and have a right to be called Christian, and so are correctly accepted as brothers by the children of the Catholic Church" (*UR* 1.3).[1] Lutheran Christians say the same of their Catholic fellow Christians.

221. Since Catholics and Lutherans are bound to one another in the body of Christ as members of it, then it is true of them what Paul says in 1 Corinthians 12:26: "If one member suffers, all suffer together; if one member is honored, all rejoice together." What affects one member of the body also affects all the others. For this reason, when Lutheran Christians remember the events that led to the particular formation of their churches, they do not wish to do so without their Catholic fellow Christians. In remembering with each other the beginning of the Reformation, they are taking their baptism seriously.

222. Because they believe that they belong to the one body of Christ, Lutherans emphasize that their church did not originate with the Refor-

---

1. www.vatican.va/archive/hist_councils/ii_vatican_council/documents/vat-ii_decree_19641121_unitatis-redintegratio_en.html.

mation or come into existence only 500 years ago. Rather, they are convinced that the Lutheran churches have their origin in the Pentecost event and the proclamation of the apostles. Their churches obtained their particular form, however, through the teaching and efforts of the reformers. The reformers had no desire to found a new church, and according to their own understanding, they did not do so. They wanted to reform the church, and they managed to do so within their field of influence, albeit with errors and missteps.

PREPARING FOR COMMEMORATION

223. As members of one body, Catholics and Lutherans remember together the events of the Reformation that led to the reality that thereafter they lived in divided communities even though they still belonged to one body. That is an impossible possibility and the source of great pain. Because they belong to one body, Catholics and Lutherans struggle in the face of their division toward the full catholicity of the church. This struggle has two sides: the recognition of what is common and joins them together, and the recognition of what divides. The first is reason for gratitude and joy; the second is reason for pain and lament.

224. In 2017, when Lutheran Christians celebrate the anniversary of the beginning of the Reformation, they are not thereby celebrating the division of the Western church. No one who is theologically responsible can celebrate the division of Christians from one another.

Shared joy in the gospel

225. Lutherans are thankful in their hearts for what Luther and the other reformers made accessible to them: the understanding of the gospel of Jesus Christ and faith in him; the insight into the mystery of the Triune God who gives Himself to us human beings out of grace and who can be received only in full trust in the divine promise; in the freedom and certainty that the gospel creates; in the love that comes from and is awakened by faith, and in the hope in life and death that faith brings with it; and in the living contact with the Holy Scripture, the catechisms, and hymns that draw faith into life. Remembrance and

present commemoration will add additional reasons to be thankful to this list. This gratitude is what makes Lutheran Christians want to celebrate in 2017.

226. Lutherans also realize that what they are thanking God for is not a gift that they can claim only for themselves. They want to share this gift with all other Christians. For this reason they invite all Christians to celebrate with them. As the previous chapter has shown, Catholics and Lutherans have so much of the faith in common that they can—and in fact should—be thankful together, especially on the day of commemoration of the Reformation.

227. This takes up an impulse that the Second Vatican Council expressed: "Catholics must gladly acknowledge and esteem the truly Christian endowments from our common heritage which are to be found among our separated brethren. It is right and salutary to recognize the riches of Christ and virtuous works in the lives of others who are bearing witness to Christ, sometimes even to the shedding of their blood. For God is always wonderful in His works and worthy of all praise" (*UR* 1.4).

Reasons to regret and lament

228. As the commemoration in 2017 brings joy and gratitude to expression, so must it also allow room for both Lutherans and Catholics to experience the pain over failures and trespasses, guilt and sin in the persons and events that are being remembered.

229. On this occasion, Lutherans will also remember the vicious and degrading statements that Martin Luther made against the Jews. They are ashamed of them and deeply deplore them. Lutherans have come to recognize with a deep sense of regret the persecution of Anabaptists by Lutheran authorities and the fact that Martin Luther and Philip Melanchthon theologically supported this persecution. They deplore Luther's violent attacks against the peasants during the Peasants' War. The awareness of the dark sides of Luther and the Reformation has prompted a critical and self-critical attitude of Lutheran theologians towards Luther and the Wittenberg Reformation. Even though they agree in part with Luther's criticism of the papacy, nevertheless Lutherans today reject Luther's identification of the pope with the Antichrist.

Prayer for unity

230. Because Jesus Christ before his death prayed to the Father "that they may be one," it is clear that a division of the body of Christ is opposed to the will of the Lord. It contradicts also the express apostolic admonition that we hear in Ephesians 4:3–6: be "eager to maintain the unity of the Spirit in the bond of peace. There is one body and one Spirit—just as you were called to the one hope that belongs to your call—one Lord, one faith, one baptism, one God and Father of all, who is over all and through all and in all." The division of the body of Christ is opposed to the will of God.

Evaluating the past

231. When Catholics and Lutherans remember together the theological controversies and the events of the sixteenth century from this perspective, they must consider the circumstances of the sixteenth century. Lutherans and Catholics cannot be blamed for everything that transpired since some events in the sixteenth century were beyond their control. In the sixteenth century, theological convictions and power politics were frequently interwoven with one another. Many politicians often used genuine theological ideas to attain their ends, while many theologians promoted their theological judgments by political means. In this complex arena of numerous factors, it is difficult to ascribe responsibility for the effects of specific actions to individual persons and to name them as the guilty parties.

232. Sixteenth-century divisions were rooted in different understandings of the truth of the Christian faith and were particularly contentious since salvation was seen to be at stake. On both sides, persons held theological convictions that they could not abandon. One must not blame someone for following his or her conscience when it is formed by the Word of God and has reached its judgments after serious deliberation with others.

233. How theologians presented their theological convictions in the battle for public opinion is quite another matter. In the sixteenth century, Catholics and Lutherans frequently not only misunderstood but also exaggerated and caricatured their opponents in order to make them look ridiculous. They repeatedly violated the eighth commandment,

which prohibits bearing false witness against one's neighbor. Even if the opponents were sometimes intellectually fair to one another, their willingness to hear the other and to take his concerns seriously was insufficient. The controversialists wanted to refute and overcome their opponents, often deliberately exacerbating conflicts rather than seeking solutions by looking for what they held in common. Prejudices and misunderstandings played a great role in the characterization of the other side. Oppositions were constructed and handed down to the next generation. Here both sides have every reason to regret and lament the way in which they conducted their debates. Both Lutherans and Catholics bear the guilt that needs to be openly confessed in the remembrance of the events of 500 years ago.

Catholic confession of sins against unity

234. Already in his message to the imperial Diet in Nuremberg on 25 November 1522, Pope Hadrian VI complained of abuses and trespasses, sins and errors insofar as church authorities had committed them. Much later, during the last century, Pope Paul VI, in his opening speech at the second session of the Second Vatican Council, asked pardon from God and the divided "brethren" of the East. This gesture of the pope found expression in the Council itself, above all in the Decree on Ecumenism[2] and in the Declaration on the Relationship of the Church to Non-Christian Religions (*Nostra Acetate*).[3]

235. In a Lenten sermon, "Day of Pardon," Pope John Paul II similarly acknowledged guilt and offered prayers for forgiveness as part of the observance of the 2000 Holy Year.[4] He was the first not simply to repeat the regret of his predecessors Paul VI and the council fathers regarding the painful memories, but actually to do something about it. He also related the request for forgiveness to the office of bishop

---

2. "So we humbly beg pardon of God and of our separated brethren, just as we forgive them that trespass against us" (*UR* 7).

3. "Furthermore, in her rejection of every persecution against any man, the Church, mindful of the patrimony she shares with the Jews and moved not by political reasons but by the Gospel's spiritual love, decries hatred, persecutions, displays of anti-Semitism, directed against Jews at any time and by anyone" (*NA* 4).

4. John Paul II, "Day of Pardon," 12 March 2000, at www.vatican.va/holy_father/john _paul_ii/homilies/2000/documents/hf_jp-ii_hom_20000312_pardon_en.html.

of Rome. In his encyclical *Ut Unum Sint*, he alludes to his visit to the World Council of Churches in Geneva on 12 June 1984, admitting, "the Catholic conviction that in the ministry of the bishop of Rome she has preserved in fidelity to the Apostolic Tradition and faith of the Fathers, the visible sign and guarantor of unity constitutes a difficulty for most other Christians, whose memory is marked by certain painful recollections." He then added, "As far as we are responsible for these, I join with my predecessor Paul VI in asking forgiveness."[5]

Lutheran confession of sins against unity

236. At its fifth Assembly in Evian in 1970, the Lutheran World Federation declared in response to a deeply moving presentation by Jan Cardinal Willebrands "that we as Lutheran Christians and congregations [are] prepared to acknowledge that the judgment of the Reformers upon the Roman Catholic Church and its theology was not entirely free of po-lemical distortions, which in part have been perpetuated to the present day. We are truly sorry for the offense and misunderstanding which these polemic elements have caused our Roman Catholic brethren. We remember with gratitude the statement of Pope Paul VI to the Second Vatican Council in which he communicates his plea for forgiveness for any offense caused by the Roman Catholic Church. As we together with all Christians pray for forgiveness in the prayer our Lord has taught us, let us strive for clear, honest, and charitable language in all our conversations."[6]

237. Lutherans also confessed their wrongdoings with respect to other Christian traditions. At its eleventh Assembly in Stuttgart in 2010, the Lutheran World Federation declared that Lutherans "are filled with a deep sense of regret and pain over the persecution of Anabaptists by Lutheran authorities and especially over the fact that Lutheran reform-ers theologically supported this persecution. Thus, the Lutheran World Federation . . . wishes to express publicly its deep regret and sorrow. Trusting in God who in Jesus Christ was reconciling the world to him-self, we ask for forgiveness—from God and from our Mennonite sisters

---

5. John Paul II, *Ut Unum Sint*, 25 May 1995, 88.

6. Jan Willebrands, "Lecture to the 5th Assembly of the Lutheran World Federation, on 15 July 1970," in *La Documentation Catholique* (6 September 1970), 766.

and brothers—for the harm that our forebears in the sixteenth century committed to Anabaptists, for forgetting or ignoring this persecution in the intervening centuries, and for all inappropriate, misleading and hurtful portraits of Anabaptists and Mennonites made by Lutheran authors, in both popular and scholarly forms, to the present day."[7]

7. "Action on the Legacy of Lutheran Persecution of 'Anabaptists,'" at https://ecumenism .net/archive/docu/2010_lwf_action_legacy_lutheran_persecution_anabaptists.pdf.

Five Ecumenical Imperatives

238. Catholics and Lutherans realize that they and the communities in which they live out their faith belong to the one body of Christ. The awareness is dawning on Lutherans and Catholics that the struggle of the sixteenth century is over. The reasons for mutually condemning each other's faith have fallen by the wayside. Thus, Lutherans and Catholics identify five imperatives as they commemorate 2017 together.

239. Lutherans and Catholics are invited to think from the perspective of the unity of Christ's body and to seek whatever will bring this unity to expression and serve the community of the body of Christ. Through baptism they recognize each other mutually as Christians. This orientation requires a continual conversion of heart.

> The first imperative: Catholics and Lutherans should always begin from the perspective of unity and not from the point of view of division in order to strengthen what is held in common even though the differences are more easily seen and experienced.

240. The Catholic and Lutheran confessions have in the course of history defined themselves against one another and suffered the one-sidedness that has persisted until today when they grapple with certain problems, such as that of authority. Since the problems originated from the conflict with one another, they can only be solved or at least addressed through common efforts to deepen and strengthen their communion. Catholics and Lutherans need each other's experience, encouragement, and critique.

> The second imperative: Lutherans and Catholics must let themselves continuously be transformed by the encounter with the other and by the mutual witness of faith.

241. Catholics and Lutherans have through dialogue learned a great deal and come to appreciate the fact that communion among them can have different forms and degrees. With respect to 2017, they should renew their effort with gratitude for what has already been accomplished, with patience and perseverance since the road may be longer than expected, with eagerness that does not allow for being satisfied with the present situation, with love for one another even in times of disagreement and conflict, with faith in the Holy Spirit, with hope that the Spirit will fulfill Jesus' prayer to the Father, and with earnest prayer that this may happen.

> The third imperative: Catholics and Lutherans should again commit themselves to seek visible unity, to elaborate together what this means in concrete steps, and to strive repeatedly toward this goal.

242. Catholics and Lutherans have the task of disclosing afresh to fellow members the understanding of the gospel and the Christian faith as well as previous church traditions. Their challenge is to prevent this rereading of tradition from falling back into the old confessional oppositions.

> The fourth imperative: Lutherans and Catholics should jointly rediscover the power of the gospel of Jesus Christ for our time.

243. Ecumenical engagement for the unity of the church does not serve only the church but also the world so that the world may believe. The missionary task of ecumenism will become greater the more pluralistic our societies become with respect to religion. Here again a rethinking and metanoia are required.

> The fifth imperative: Catholics and Lutherans should witness together to the mercy of God in proclamation and service to the world.

244. The ecumenical journey enables Lutherans and Catholics to appreciate together Martin Luther's insight into and spiritual experience of the gospel of the righteousness of God, which is also God's mercy. In the preface to his Latin works (1545), he noted that "by the mercy of God, meditating day and night," he gained new understanding of Romans 1:17: "here I felt that I was altogether born again and had entered paradise itself through open gates. Thereupon a totally other face of the entire Scripture showed itself to me. . . . Later I read Augustine's The Spirit and the Letter, where contrary to hope I found that he, too, interpreted God's righteousness in a similar way, as the righteousness with which God clothes us when he justifies us."[1]

245. The beginnings of the Reformation will be rightly remembered when Lutherans and Catholics hear together the gospel of Jesus Christ and allow themselves to be called anew into community with the Lord. Then they will be united in a common mission which the *Joint Declaration on the Doctrine of Justification* describes: "Lutherans and Catholics share the goal of confessing Christ in all things, who alone is to be trusted above all things as the one Mediator (1 Tim. 2:5f) through whom God in the Holy Spirit gives himself and pours out his renewing gifts" (*JDDJ* 18).

---

1. Luther, "Preface to the Complete Edition of Luther's Latin Writings," tr. Lewis W. Spitz, Sr., in *LW* 34:337; *WA* 54; 186, 3.8–10.16–18.

Abbreviations

AAS	Acta Apostolicae Sedis
ApC	*The Apostolicity of the Church: Study Document of the Lutheran–Roman Catholic Commission on Unity* (2006)
Apol.	Apology of the Augsburg Confession (1530)
AS	Smalcald Articles (1537)
BC	*The Book of Concord: The Confessions of the Evangelical Lutheran Church*
BSLK	*Die Bekenntnisschriften der evangelisch-lutherischen Kirche* (Göttingen, 1930; 10th ed. 1986)
CA	Augsburg Confession
can.	Canon
CD	Vatican II: Decree on the Pastoral Office of Bishops in the Church, *Christus Dominus*
DH	H. Denzinger and P. Hünermann (eds), *Enchiridion symbolorum definitionum et declarationum de rebus fidei et morum* (Freiburg, 2001)
DV	Vatican II: Dogmatic Constitution *Dei Verbum*
Epit.	Epitome (Formula of Concord)
Eucharist	*The Eucharist: Final Report of the Joint Roman Catholic–Lutheran Commission* (1978)
FC	Formula of Concord (1577)
JDDJ	*Joint Declaration on the Doctrine of Justification* (1999)
LC	M. Luther, Large Catechism (1529)
LG	Vatican II: Dogmatic Constitution on the Church, *Lumen Gentium*
LW	*Luther's Works*, American Edition, ed. J. Pelikan and H. T. Lehmann, 54 vols (Philadelphia and St. Louis, 1955–1986)

LWF	The Lutheran World Federation
Ministry	*Ministry in the Church,* Lutheran–Roman Catholic Conversation, 1981
PO	Vatican II: Decree on the Ministry and Life of Priests, *Presbyterorum Ordinis*
SC	Vatican II: Constitution on the Sacred Liturgy, *Sacrosanctum Concilium*
SmC	M. Luther, Small Catechism (1529)
STh	Thomas Aquinas, *Summa Theologiae,* Latin/Engl., Blackfriars (London and New York, 1963)
UR	Vatican II: Decree on Ecumenism, *Unitatis Redintegratio*
WA	M. Luther, *Werke* (Weimar, 1883ff.) (Weimarer Ausgabe)

Statements and Membership of the Lutheran–Roman Catholic Commission on Unity

COMMON STATEMENTS

PHASE I (1967–1972)

The Gospel and the Church (Malta Report—1972)

PHASE II (1973–1984)

The Eucharist (1978)
All under One Christ (1980)
Ways to Community (1980)
The Ministry in the Church (1981)
Martin Luther—Witness to Christ (1983)
Facing Unity—Models, Forms and Phases of Catholic-Lutheran Church Fellowship (1984)

PHASE III (1986–1993)

Church and Justification (1993)

PHASE IV (1995–2006)

Joint Declaration on the Doctrine of Justification (1999—signed by representatives of the Catholic Church and the Lutheran World Federation)
The Apostolicity of the Church (2006)

MEMBERS OF THE COMMISSION

LUTHERANS

Members	Bishop emeritus Dr. Eero Huovinen (Co-Chair), Finland
	Rev. Prof. Dr. Wanda Deifelt, Brazil
	Dr. Sandra Gintere, Latvia
	Prof. Dr. Turid Karlsen Seim, Norway
	Rev. Dr. Fidon R. Mwombeki, Tanzania
	Prof. Dr. Friederike Nüssel, Germany
	Prof. Dr. Michael Root, USA (2009)
	Rev. Prof. Dr. Hiroshi Augustine Suzuki, Japan
	Rev. Prof. Dr. Ronald F. Thiemann, USA (2010–)
Consultant	Rev. Prof. Dr. Theodor Dieter, Institute for Ecumenical Research, Strasbourg
Staff	Prof. Dr. Kathryn L. Johnson, Co-Secretary, The Luther World Federation

ROMAN CATHOLICS

Members	Bishop Prof. Dr. Gerhard Ludwig Müller (Co-Chair), Germany (2009–2012)
	Bishop Prof. Dr. Kurt Koch, Switzerland (2009)
	Auxiliary Bishop Prof. Dr. Karlheinz Diez, Germany (2012–)
	Rev. Prof. Dr. Michel Fédou, SJ, France
	Rev. Prof. Dr. Angelo Maffeis, Italy
	Prof. Dr. Thomas Söding, Germany
	Prof. Dr. Christian D. Washburn, USA
	Prof. Dr. Susan K. Wood, SCL, USA
Consultants	Prof. Dr. Eva-Maria Faber, Switzerland
	Prof. Dr. Wolfgang Thönissen, Johann-Adam-Möhler-Institut für Ökumenik, Germany
Staff	Mons. Dr. Matthias Türk, Co-Secretary, Pontifical Council for Promoting Christian Unity

A Study Guide to
From Conflict to Communion

*by the Planning Committee of the Roman Catholic
Diocese of Pittsburgh*

and the Roman Catholic Diocese of Greensburg,

the Byzantine Catholic Archeparchy of Pittsburgh,

*and the Southwestern Pennsylvania Synod
of the Evangelical Lutheran Church of America*

Introduction

All of us come to *From Conflict to Communion* and this study guide with a personal history that includes our spiritual journey. Our hope is that this history will enrich our prayer together and our discussions.

We may, however, also bring with us some unresolved feelings about ecumenical dialogue and/or about Lutherans or Catholics we have known. The study may turn out to be a time for identifying past incidents or choices and attendant emotions.

The study guide is designed to increase mutual understanding between Catholics, Lutherans, and other friends. It may also be a catalyst for healing and reconciliation communally and individually.

This study guide for *From Conflict to Communion* is intended to assist group discussion of this important common commemoration of the Reformation. As noted in the foreword, "In 2017, Catholics and Lutheran Christians will most fittingly look back on events that occurred 500 years earlier by putting the gospel of Jesus Christ at the center." In order to affirm that center, we are called to take a critical look at how each of our traditions contributed to the loss of unity in Western Christendom. The goal of our mutual commemoration must include remembering our history and continuing our movement toward the unity that Christ wills for His followers.

The study guide begins with prayers for use at the beginning of each section. It then reviews the foreword to *From Conflict to Communion* and the three points in the Introduction, followed by the consideration of The Five Ecumenical Imperatives (chapter six). Those who engage with the text will find it helpful to focus on the fundamentals first, in order to go deeper, rather than reading it from cover to cover. The beginning discussion in the first session will help set the tone for looking at the chapters of *From Conflict to Communion*. Sessions may be adjusted and combined as planned.

Beginning with Prayer

Prior to the start of each session, and after appropriate introductions have been made, begin each session with prayer. Then pause for a time of silent reflection.

PRAYERS

Several prayers are offered below. As collegiality develops and the local context is defined, specific prayers and intercession might be offered during this time.

God our Father, your Son Jesus prayed that his followers might be one. Make all Christians one with him as he is one with you, so that in peace and concord we may carry to the world the message of your love, through Jesus Christ, our Savior and Lord. (*Evangelical Lutheran Worship*, 2006)

Gracious Father, we pray for your holy catholic church. Fill it with all truth and peace. Where it is corrupt, purify it; where it is in error, direct it; where in anything it is amiss, reform it; where it is right, strengthen it; where it is in need, provide for it; where it is divided, reunite it; for the sake of Jesus Christ, your Son, our Lord. (*Evangelical Lutheran Worship*, 2006)

Most high and holy God, pour out upon us your one and unifying Spirit, and awaken in every confession of the whole church a holy hunger and thirst for unity in you; through Jesus Christ, our Savior and Lord. (*Evangelical Lutheran Worship*, 2006)

For all kinds of Christians we are grateful, acknowledging the Spirit's work in our distinctions, and praying for the grace to perceive the divisiveness that pride creates. In that we are separated sisters and brothers by reason of our own fault, perpetuating the sins of the centuries: Forgive us dear Lord, and unite us in your love. (Carl T. Uehling, *The Wideness of God's Mercy*, Vol. 1, 1985)

God of our lives, by the power of your Holy Spirit we have been drawn together by one baptism into one faith serving one Lord and Savior. Do not let us tear away from one another through division or hard argument. May your peace embrace our differences, preserving us in unity, as one body of Jesus Christ our Lord. (*Book of Common Worship*, Westminster John Knox Press, 1993)

Holy God, giver of peace, author of truth, we confess that we are divided and at odds with one another, that a bad spirit has risen among us and set us against your Holy Spirit of peace and love. Take from us the mistrust, party spirit, contention, and all evil that now divides us. Work in us a desire for reconciliation, so that, putting aside personal grievances, we may go about your business with a single mind, devoted to our Lord and Savior, Jesus Christ. (Dionysius of Alexandria, d. 264. *Book of Common Worship*, Westminster John Knox Press, 1993)

Almighty, ever-living God, who gather what is scattered and keep together what you have gathered, look kindly on the flock of your Son, that those whom one Baptism has consecrated may be joined together by integrity of faith and united always in the bond of charity. Through our Lord Jesus Christ, your Son, who lives and reigns with you in the unity of the Holy Spirit, one God, forever and ever. (Mass for Unity of Christians, Collect A)

Attend with favor to the prayers of your people, we ask, O Lord, and grant that the hearts of believers may be united in your praise and in repentance together, so that, with division among Christians overcome, we may hasten with joy to your eternal Kingdom in perfect communion of the Church. Through Jesus Christ our Lord. (Mass for Unity of Christians, Collect B)

Look with favor on your people, Lord, we pray, and pour out upon them the gifts of your Spirit, that they may grow constantly in love of the truth and devote themselves with zeal to perfect unity among Christians. Through our Lord Jesus Christ, your Son, who lives and reigns with you in the unity of the Holy Spirit, one God forever and ever. (Mass for Unity of Christians, Collect C)

Heavenly Father, we come to you, the Font of Life, to ask that you fill your Church with Living Water to quench our thirst on the quest for Christian unity. Let our hearts be filled with the gift of your Son's love for us. May we find in your Church the living and abiding presence of your love and work together to bring about the desire of your Son, Our Lord Jesus Christ when he prayed, "that they all may be one." May the Spirit never lay dormant within us, but sustain us on the path of life. This we ask through Jesus Christ, our Lord, who lives and reigns with you, in the unity of the Holy Spirit, one God, now and forever. Amen. (Prayer for Week of Christian Unity 2015).

FOR REFLECTION

It is the task of every Christian to build the unity of the Church. When constructing a temple or a building, the first thing one does is find suitable land. Then one lays the cornerstone, the Bible says. And the cornerstone of the unity of the Church, or rather the cornerstone of the Church, is Jesus and the cornerstone of the unity of the Church is Jesus' prayer at the Last Supper: "Father, that they may be one!" And this is its strength! Humility, gentleness, magnanimity: These are weak things, because the humble person appears good for nothing; gentleness, meekness appear useless; generosity, being open to all, having a big heart. The weaker we are with these virtues of humility, generosity, gentleness, meekness, the stronger we become as stones in this Temple. We have been called to a great hope. Let's go there, but with the strength that Jesus' prayer for unity gives us; with docility to the Holy Spirit, who is capable of making living stones from bricks; and with the hope of finding the Lord who has called us, to encounter Him in the fullness of time. (Homily of Pope Francis, October 24, 2014)

Foreword and Introduction

The first session covers the foreword and the introduction to *From Conflict to Communion*.

THE FOREWORD

Read the foreword, then discuss:

After reading the foreword in its entirety, discuss the following:

1. How is Martin Luther's life characterized? What is the central theme?
   a. Do you think this is a fair characterization? Why or why not?
   b. How does being Catholic or Lutheran color our image of Luther?
   c. Is Luther's statement: "**True theology and the knowledge of God are in the crucified Christ**" a place that both Catholics and Lutherans can rest in regardless of one's thought on the person of Luther? Explain.

2. If it is true that "**both as individuals and as a community of believers, we all constantly require repentance and reform—encouraged and led by the Holy Spirit**" how might this be a rallying point for a commemoration of the 500th anniversary of 1517?

3. Review the Joint Declaration on the Doctrine of Justification. What is the shared understanding of justification articulated in the document?

4. Discuss the two challenges identified as integral to the commemorative year:
   a. . . . **the purification and healing of memories**
   b. . . . **and the restoration of Christian unity in accordance with the truth of the gospel of Jesus Christ** (Eph. 4:4–6)
   c. Offer some initial thoughts about what comes to mind when you read and hear these two goals. Do any practical resolutions of how these might be achieved, or at least worked toward, come to mind? If so please share them with the group. After this is completed ask someone to offer a prayer of petition and thanksgiving that these two general goals may become a reality through our continued conversion of heart and mind in docility to the Holy Spirit.

The Introduction

Read the introduction, then discuss:

1. Before delving into the question of Martin Luther as witness to Jesus Christ, ask everyone in the group to express in their own words what it means to be a "witness for Jesus Christ."

2. a. After this is completed spend some time discussing Martin Luther—How was and is he a witness to Jesus Christ? What areas did he excel in doing this? In what ways did he perhaps need to continue to grow?
   b. For silent reflection or to share with the group if so desired: In what ways do I excel as a witness? In what ways do I need to continue to grow?

Chapter VI: Five Ecumenical Imperatives

It may seem strange to skip to chapter six in the study guide, but the ecumenical imperatives are very important in studying *From Conflict to Communion* and moving to a new understanding of our life together as Christians.

1. Read paragraphs 238–239 and the First Imperative, then discuss:
    a. Why is it important to realize that we belong to the One Body of Christ?
    b. Do we accept one another's baptism? Why is this important?
    c. Do you feel relieved that we no longer condemn the faith of other Christians? Does this mean that we no longer have differences? How can we lift this up as an alternative voice/face of Christianity?
    d. How does it make a difference that we begin from a perspective of unity and not from the point of view of division?
    e. Share any additional observations about this imperative.

2. Read paragraph 240 and the Second Imperative, then discuss:
    a. Through the years, Catholics and Lutherans shared in their confessional writings that they were right and the other was wrong in many matters of faith and theology. With a renewed goal of looking toward unity, it is essential to re-visit these problem areas and assess whether what has been written should be rejected, discussed further, or re-evaluated in order to resolve the differences. Why is it important that we remain patient so that our national and international Lutheran-Catholic dialogues can address differences, as well as consensus agreements?
    b. What do you believe it means to be transformed by the encounter with the other and by mutual witness of faith? How would this

make a difference as we relate to one another even when there are issues of faith and life that exist?

    c. How can we become informed of agreements and continued differences?

    d. Share any additional observations about this imperative.

3. Read paragraph 241 and the Third Imperative, then discuss:

    a. Among subjects that have been addressed through the United States Conference of Catholic Bishops and the Evangelical Lutheran Church in America (and its predecessor churches) are the following: Scripture and Tradition; The Condemnations of the Reformation Era—Do They Still Divide?; The Status of the Nicene Creed as Dogma of the Church; One Baptism for the Remission of Sins; The Eucharist as Sacrifice; The One Mediator, the Saints and Mary; Teaching Authority, and the Joint Declaration on the Doctrine of Justification.

    b. Common statements in the US dialogues were developed and were widely distributed and embraced. There has been an observation that many people are not aware of the statements and agreements, especially those who have not followed developments or who came after the statements were made. Do you believe that the 500th Anniversary would be a good time to become aware of these statements? What would be the advantages of studying them?

    c. Share any additional observations about this imperative.

4. Read paragraph 242 and the Fourth Imperative, then discuss:

    a. The power of the Gospel of Jesus Christ brings good news to a world that God continues to love and redeem. What would be helpful for you to better understand the gospel and the Christian faith as well as previous church traditions?

    b. Do you believe it is important for Lutherans and Catholics to make a joint faith witness that would share the good news of the life, death, and resurrection of our Lord Jesus Christ? How would you support this type of witness? What would be your concerns?

    c. Share any additional observations about this imperative.

5. Read paragraph 243 and the Fifth Imperative, then discuss:

    a. The Christian faith is often described as irrelevant by people who are outside the church or who have left active membership in the church. Jesus wanted the world to believe so He prayed for the unity of His followers. What are some of the ways in which Lutherans and Catholics could show unity that would attract the attention and possible outreach to non-church persons?

   b. How is the mercy of God seen in your daily life? In your area? In the world? Are there advantages of joining hands as fellow Christians in sharing God's mercy to a world in need?

6. Read paragraphs 244–245, then discuss:
   a. Could you affirm Luther's faith insights that are highlighted in paragraph 244?
   b. How does Scripture inform your faith and life?
   c. Paragraph 245 contains some hopeful words and an invitation about hearing and being called. How do you understand what we are to hear together? How can this be done? Do you believe that it is our Lord's will that we be united in a common mission? Whose mission would it be? How might we discern such a mission together?

Chapter I: Commemorating the Reformation in an Ecumenical and Global Age

1. Read paragraph 4, then discuss:
   a. This paragraph deals with "context." Have each person in the group choose one of the three listed challenges—the one that most "grabs" them—and have them briefly elaborate on what it is that captures their imagination about this particular challenge
   b. and/or, if anybody wants to add one of their own that they think has been overlooked they are invited to do so.

2. Read paragraphs 5–6, "The Character of Previous Commemorations," then discuss:
   a. How have commemorations been handled in the past?
   b. Perhaps a few members of the group can relate personal experiences of how they have commemorated this in the past.

3. Read paragraphs 7–9, "The First Ecumenical Commemoration," then discuss:
   a. What changes have come about in the past 50 years that will allow Catholics and Lutherans to commemorate 1517 differently in 2017?
   b. "These changes demand a new approach" is the first line of paragraph 8. Building on what has already been discussed, are there "new approaches" that have already come into existence that you wish to praise or perhaps there are some which you hope to see come into existence? Discuss these.
   c. Even when oppositional differences remain, what can we learn from 50 years of dialogue, prayer, and worship?
   d. Reread this paragraph aloud before discussing. In your own words what are the two points of departure? Is it possible to take **both**

points of departure seriously as recommended by the document? Practice this in the group. What can each person affirm about both the Catholic and Lutheran positions?

4. Read paragraphs 10–12, "Commemoration in a New Global and Secular Context," then discuss:
   a. What experiences do you have with the globalized Church mentioned in paragraph 10? In what ways has the development of a global church and Christianity helped to change the context of the confessional conflicts of history? How might these influences impact 2017?
   b. What do you think the last line of paragraph 11 means? "As a result of this forgetting, much of what divided the church in the past is virtually unknown today." Does the receding of Christian influence actually present an ecumenical opportunity?
   c. Paragraph 12 is a tough one! Even while we lament the divisions of the past this statement invites us to think about what was and is at the heart of the Confessional disagreements. What was and is at the heart? "How can the traditions be passed on in such a way that they do not dig new trenches between Christians of different confessions?" In short—can our ecumenical work be incorporated into our particular traditions and become part of what we hand on? Is ecumenism a part of authentic Christian witnessing?

5. Read paragraphs 13–15, "New Challenges for the 2017 Commemoration," then discuss:
   a. This could be a wide-ranging discussion, but take some time to discuss the intersection of the culture and the church. In what ways does culture still reflect Christ and Christianity? In what ways have they parted or exist in opposition to each other?
   b. In a similar vein to paragraph 11, how have certain trends perhaps made "old confessional controversies seem obsolete"? Specifically with regard to the phenomena of charismatic churches?
   c. It is a new time and a new era—how will the contemporary world impact the Commemoration of 2017?

Chapter II: New Perspectives
on Martin Luther and the Reformation

Read paragraphs 16–17, then discuss:

Why is it important to recognize the "commonalities within the differences" of our respective faiths? Discuss some beliefs Catholics and Lutherans have in common.

ECUMENICAL PROJECTS PREPARING THE WAY
FOR CONSENSUS

Read paragraphs 18–25, then discuss:

What conclusions might you draw from the research of Catholic scholars in the twentieth century regarding Martin Luther and the Reformation? How might this affect your outlook toward each other's church/religion?

CATHOLIC DEVELOPMENTS

Read paragraphs 26–27, then discuss briefly the themes of Vatican Council II listed below and share your experiences and understanding of each:

Esteem and reverence for the Holy Scripture in the life of the church
What role does Holy Scripture play in your life? Discuss some similarities between Catholics and Lutherans regarding the use of Holy Scripture. (Vatican Council II, *Revelation*, Chapter VI, "Sacred Scripture in the Life of the Church")

Rediscovery of the common priesthood of all the baptized

Do you recognize your part in the common priesthood? How does this play out in your daily dealings with others? Is it difficult to speak about your faith with other Catholics/Lutherans or non-Christians? (Vatican Council II, *The Church*, Chapter I, "The Mystery of the Church," Article 15)

Need for continual purification and reform of the church

How has Vatican Council II impacted your attitude for our understanding of each other's beliefs? How important is participation in Liturgy for you as a Catholic or Lutheran? (Vatican Council II, *Ecumenism*)

Understanding of church office as service

At his installation as head of the Catholic Church, Pope Francis stated that we should "Never forget that authentic power is service" and that "Only those who serve with love are able to protect." Discuss what meaning these two statements might have for you as faithful followers of Christ.

Importance of the freedom and responsibility of human beings, including the recognition of religious freedom

Discuss how the following statements of Vatican Council II impact your understanding of discipleship. What is the Church's divine mission?

- Vatican Council II informs us that "As the spiritual authority appointed by Christ, with the duty imposed by divine command, of going into the whole world and preaching the Gospel to every creature, the Church claims freedom for herself in human society and before every public authority." (Vatican Council II, *Declaration on Religious Liberty*, Chapter II, "Religious Freedom in the Light of Revelation," Article 13)
- "When the principle of religious freedom is not just proclaimed in words or incorporated in law, but is implemented sincerely in practice, only then does the church enjoy in law and in fact, those stable conditions which give her the independence necessary for fulfilling her divine mission." (Vatican Council II, *Declaration on Religious Liberty*, Chapter II, "Religious Freedom in the Light of Revelation," Article 13)
- "(We) must take into account (our) duties toward Christ, the life-giving Word whom (we) must proclaim, the rights of the human person, and the measure of grace which God has given to each (of us) through Christ in calling (us) freely to accept and profess the faith."

(Vatican Council II, *Declaration on Religious Liberty*, Chapter II, "Religious Freedom in the Light of Revelation," Article 14)

Read paragraphs 28–29, then discuss:

Paragraph 28 states that as a result of Vatican Council II "Catholics today can appreciate Martin Luther's reforming concerns and regard them with more openness."

- How do you as a Catholic or Lutheran relate to this statement?
- Do you see a need for dialogue among members of both traditions? What would you hope to gain from such dialogue/encounters?
- Do you agree with the statement in paragraph 29, that Luther's "intention was to reform, not to divide, the church"? Discuss some of the positive and negative things about Catholics or Lutherans that you learned as a child/young person from others: parents, grandparents, friends etc.

Read paragraph 30, then discuss:

- How do you relate to Pope Benedict's statement about Luther regarding the question of God? What does the question of God mean in *your* life?
- Do you agree that "most people today, even Christians, set out from the presupposition that God is not fundamentally interested in our sins and virtues"? Why or why not?

LUTHERAN DEVELOPMENTS

Read paragraph 31, then discuss:

As a result of Vatican Council II and the historical, social, and theological factors regarding Luther and the Reformation, Catholic and Lutheran theologians are now in dialogue about the commonalities and differences of their respective traditions. Would you agree that some progress has been made here? Do you think future progress toward full unity is possible? Why or why not?

THE IMPORTANCE OF ECUMENICAL DIALOGUES

Read paragraphs 32–34, then discuss:

Share your thoughts about the following statements:

- "In order to determine the exact relationship between respective articles of doctrine, texts must be interpreted in the light of the historical context in which they arose. That allows one to see where a difference or opposition truly exists and where it does not."
- "Ecumenical dialogue is the common search for the truth of the Christian faith."

For additional reading regarding Catholic-Lutheran dialogue see: Walter Cardinal Kasper, *Harvesting the Fruits: Basic Aspects of Christian Faith in Ecumenical Dialogue* (New York: Continuum, 2009).

Chapter III: A Historical Sketch of the Lutheran Reformation and the Catholic Response

WHAT DOES REFORMATION MEAN?

Read paragraphs 35–39, then discuss:

- Give an illustration of how two different parties might remember a particular event. Why is it important to "find a common way of re-membering past events"?
- When you think about the term "Reformation," what thoughts and feelings come to mind? Is the term a positive, negative, or neutral one for you?

CONTROVERSY OVER INDULGENCES

Read paragraphs 40–42, then discuss:

- What was one abuse which Luther identified in the issuing of indul-gences during his time? What other indulgence-related questions did Luther have? How do we address and understand these issues today?
- What problem do you think may have been caused by the broad pub-lication of the 95 Theses, as opposed to confining them to the context of academic theological discussion?

LUTHER ON TRIAL, FAILED ENCOUNTERS, AND THE CONDEMNATION OF MARTIN LUTHER

Read paragraphs 43–51, then discuss:

- Why was the Vatican alarmed by the broad publication of the theses? How does fear inhibit our ability to hear and understand one another?
- #45: *"Cardinal Cajetan was given the mandate to interrogate Luther. . . . Luther was to recant or . . . the Cardinal had the power to ban Luther . . . or to arrest him and bring him to Rome." #46: "Luther was promised a fair trial. Nevertheless . . . , he repeatedly received the message that he either had to recant or be proclaimed a heretic."* These statements imply that Luther's treatment was anything but fair. Is it surprising to you that this appears in a jointly written document? Why is it important to talk about the "hard things" in ecumenical discussion?

THE AUTHORITY OF SCRIPTURE AND LUTHER IN WORMS

Read paragraphs 52–57, then discuss:

- It is a **caricature** to say that Lutherans adhere to the authority of the Bible alone and Roman Catholics submit to the authority of the pope alone. Is this caricature still alive? Give examples which dispel it.

BEGINNINGS OF THE REFORMATION MOVEMENT

Read paragraphs 58–61, then discuss:

- *Roman Catholics:* Do you recognize your experience in any of the changes described in these paragraphs? What is still foreign? *Lutherans:* Do you see yourself participating in the ongoing reform of the Church? If so, how?

Bringing the Scripture to the People, Catechisms and Hymns, and Ministers for Parishes

Read paragraphs 62–68, then discuss:

- As Lutherans and Roman Catholics, talk about your experience of a) the Bible; b) Christian education for children and adults, and the books you used; and c) the use of hymns in church services. Do we share any?
- Why did early Lutherans use pastors to ordain new pastors? Why did they consider this to be legitimate? How were (and are) these ordinations viewed by the Roman Catholic Church? What place might historical considerations play in the recognition of Lutheran ordination by the Roman Catholic Church?

Theological Attempts to Overcome the Religious Conflict

Read paragraphs 69–73, then discuss:

- The first section of the Augsburg Confession sums up doctrine which Lutherans held to be undisputed, differing only in inconsequential matters. The second part deals with matters still under dispute. What are some important areas of doctrinal agreement between Lutherans and Catholics today? Where do we still disagree? Do you see the differences which remain as truly "church dividing"?

Religious War and the Peace of Augsburg

Read paragraphs 74–77, then discuss:

- In this section we read about some details of the interplay between state and church. How might this European experience have influenced the First Amendment, which states: "Congress shall make no law respecting an establishment of religion, or prohibiting the free exercise thereof . . ."?

THE COUNCIL OF TRENT

Read paragraphs 78–89, then discuss:

- Trent rejected the *sola scriptura*, insisting that Scripture and Tradition taken together bear the fullness of the faith. Give an example of Tradition which is held as part of the faith by the Roman Catholic Church, but which does not appear explicitly in the Bible. Does this present an obstacle to Christian unity?
- Trent published an "official" list of biblical books. Examine the index of a "Protestant" and a "Catholic" Bible. Why does this list of books differ?
- Trent rejected *"the doctrine of justification by faith alone (*sola fide*), while understanding faith primarily as assent to revealed doctrine. . . . It declared the essence of justification to be not the remission of sins alone, but also the 'sanctification and renovation of the inner man' by supernatural charity"* (#82). Discuss your **personal** understanding of the term "faith." Is it intellectual belief alone or does it include something else? How does your discussion bear on the "controversy" between "faith alone," and "faith plus good works"?
- Trent defined seven sacraments. Lutherans generally recognize only two, but have rites which correspond to the other five. Discuss your understanding of baptism and eucharist from the perspective of your own tradition. Are you **sure** of what your tradition teaches? Did your dialogue partner say anything which surprised you?
- Trent taught that the Mass makes present the sacrifice of the cross, but it is *"not a repetition of the once-for-all sacrifice"* (#85). Lutherans teach that in Holy Communion we receive Christ's true body and blood, given to us for the forgiveness of sins. How might these understandings relate to one another?
- We often think that Roman Catholics focus on the Sacraments and Lutherans focus on the Word. The Council of Trent instituted formal seminaries precisely so that the Word might be proclaimed more effectively. Lutherans understand the Sacraments as "the Word made visible." Discuss your experience of Word and Sacraments as a child, and now as an adult. What is the same? Different? What can we continue to learn from one another?
- Both Trent and the Reformers defined themselves against the other. Until recently we continued to emphasize our differences rather than

our similarities. Make a list of everything you can think of which is shared by the two churches.

THE SECOND VATICAN COUNCIL

Read paragraph 90, then discuss:

- Vatican II said that *"many elements of sanctification and of truth are found"* outside of the Roman Catholic Church, and recognized those things which it shares with other Christians, such as: *"the creeds, baptism, and the Scriptures. A theology of ecclesial communion affirmed that Catholics are in a real, if imperfect, communion with all who confess Jesus Christ and are baptized."* But Vatican II was not the last word on ecumenism. For a list of international-level dialogues and more information, go to: http://tinyurl.com/LRC-World-Dialogue. For more information on US L/RC dialogue, see: http://tinyurl.com/US-dialogue. For a press release on the current round, go to: http://tinyurl.com/Current-USLRC.
- Discuss: How will you help to spread the word to the people at your church about what you are learning through the study of this document?

Chapter IV: Basic Themes of Martin Luther's Theology in Light of the Lutheran–Roman Catholic Dialogues

INTRODUCTION

This chapter examines four areas of Martin Luther's theology—justification, the Lord's Supper, Ministry and Scripture/Tradition—with some concluding remarks about ecclesiology. By focusing on Martin Luther's theology, the reader may obtain a better grasp of the origins of specific differences in teaching and the degree to which today's ecumenical conversations have helped to remove misconceptions and have grown to understand the differences between our two communions. Each of the jointly written sections contains enough information to be a chapter in itself, worthy of extended conversation among Lutherans and Roman Catholics today. Given the upcoming commemoration of the Reformation in 2017, it is important that this chapter concentrates not on Lutheran confessional writings (contained in the *Book of Concord*) but Luther's own thought (paragraph 93).

As the reader goes through this material, it is important to note its structure. It begins with a summary of Luther's perspective, followed by a brief look at Roman Catholic concerns, and concludes with an examination of a harvest of ecumenical dialogues regarding these points, keeping in mind that the authority of the ecumenical statements varies, with the *Joint Declaration on the Doctrine of Justification* having a higher authority than statements from the dialogues themselves (paragraph 97).

(1) JUSTIFICATION

A. Central to Luther's theological teaching and to the Reformation was the understanding that we are justified by God's grace through faith. Paragraph

107 emphasizes that God's love for humanity is centered in Jesus Christ so that "by grace alone" is also always "by Christ alone" where the believer's sin is exchanged for Christ's righteousness.

B. In 1999, the Joint Declaration on the Doctrine of Justification was adopted by the Vatican and the Lutheran World Federation. Both communions insisted upon God's grace alone ("the forgiving and renewing mercy that God imparts as a gift," paragraph 124) is the cause of justification. Both communions agree that this takes place by faith alone, understood as the trust based on God's Word.

1. If this joint doctrine of justification shows a differentiated consensus about how we are forgiven and saved, what does this say about how we treat one another as fellow Christians? (See paragraph 138.)
2. What do you believe is meant by the Lutheran teaching that we are both saint and sinner at the same time? (See paragraph 116.)
3. Luther had a deep commitment to the freedom of the Christian, where the freedom of God's grace and faith in God's promises in Christ result in "the freedom to serve one's neighbor spontaneously without seeking merits in doing so" (paragraph 118). Should we expect to build up merits for serving our neighbor? Is it sufficient to know that we are acting in love and not with the expectation that we are rewarded for what we do?

(2) The Eucharist

Luther understood the Lord's Supper as both a promise of Christ's presence (his true body and blood) and a testament of grace and forgiveness. In dialogue, both communions affirm Christ's real presence in the Eucharist without adopting philosophical terminology to explain it.

1. While we are not yet able to share Holy Communion, how important is it to know that we agree that we receive the Body and Blood of Christ? (Note: some Christian communions teach that in Communion it is only a spiritual presence or it is simply a memorial.)
2. How have you seen the practice of Holy Communion change in your context? Is there a more frequent reception of Communion?
3. Both Lutherans and Catholics have benefited from the liturgical move-

ment of the twentieth century (viewing the sacrament as a memorial that makes present the events of salvation; affirming other aspects of Christ's presence in the Word and in the assembly; reevaluating other expressions of Christ's real presence, learning to deal respectfully with the elements after the meal). How has the liturgy changed in your church? Do people participate more actively in worship and in the Eucharist?

(3) MINISTRY

1. Luther emphasized the priesthood of the baptized. Christ alone is high priest, and through baptism believers share his priesthood and kingship (I Peter 2:9). He also emphasized that while all are priests, not all are ministers. Do you believe every Christian is called to exercise the calling in their baptism to serve God and their neighbor?

2. In the study document, *The Apostolicity of the Church*, there was a common understanding of the priesthood of the baptized, the divine source of the ordained office of public ministry, the centrality of proclamation of the gospel and administration of the Sacraments. Discuss the affirmation that both communions agree that ministry serves the church universal, with Lutherans emphasizing the congregational assembly's direct relation to the church and with Roman Catholics agreeing that bishops, while not over other churches, must be "solicitous for the whole church" (paragraph 186) and, thus, that the Bishop of Rome is "pastor of the whole Church."

3. Paragraph 194 states, "Thus, the office of ministry presents both considerable obstacles to common understanding and also hopeful perspectives for rapprochement." How can bilateral studies affirm agreement as well as help resolve any differences?

(4) SCRIPTURE AND TRADITION

1. Luther regarded Scripture as the first principle and ultimate judge of all theological statements. For Luther, Scripture does not oppose all tradition but only "human traditions," that is traditions that undermine the message of Scripture itself. Since the Reformation, the relationship between Scripture and tradition has changed. Both Catholics

and Lutherans have concluded that different emphases in Scripture and tradition do not require maintaining the current division of the churches. Share some tradition that is important to you and to the Church. Where there are differences, can we respect the understanding of tradition by the other communion?

2. Ecumenical dialogue has emphasized "the efficacy of the Spirit-inspired biblical text" (paragraph 207) as it has operated over time in individuals and in ecclesial tradition, and has provided certainty for scriptural revelation. What is the work of the Holy Spirit in guiding and enlightening us as we study Scripture and as we look at Tradition in the church?

3. A first step toward consensus in matters of ecclesiology has come with the realization "that the doctrine of justification and the doctrine of the church belong together" (paragraph 216); by reciting a common Creed, Lutherans and Catholics place both doctrines in the work of the Trinity. Why is it helpful to note that Catholics and Lutherans confess together the faith in the one, holy, catholic and apostolic church? (See paragraph 218.)

Chapter V: Called to Common Commemoration

Baptism: The Basis for Unity and Common Commemoration

Read paragraphs 219–222, then discuss:

- Share your experiences of participating in baptisms at your own congregation. Who participated? Within the Eucharistic liturgy or separately? Describe the liturgical actions.
- Share your experiences of being a guest at a baptism performed in a congregation other than your own (for Catholics, attending a baptism at a Lutheran church; for Lutherans, attending a baptism at a Catholic church). What was similar to your own tradition? What was different? How were you welcomed or acknowledged as being a fellow member of Christ's body?
- How has your understanding of the origins and histories of Catholic and Lutheran identity changed in your lifetime?

Preparing for Commemoration

Read paragraphs 223–224, then discuss:

- Share a personal story of living "in divided communities."
- Imagine a shared Catholic-Lutheran commemoration on October 31, 2017. What attitudes might shape such a commemoration? Is there language or terms we would want to avoid?

SHARED JOY IN THE GOSPEL

Read paragraphs 225–227, then discuss:

- Share your favorite gospel story.
- Read together the most recent Lutheran and Catholic translations of the Nicene Creed. Are there differences in wording? Why? What are they attempting to say?
- What gifts do Lutherans possess that they want to share with their Catholic siblings?
- How might Catholics acknowledge the validity, virtuous works, and witness to Christ of their "separated brethren" of the Lutheran tradition?

REASONS TO REGRET AND LAMENT

Read paragraphs 228–229, then discuss:

- What is the Lutheran understanding of "simultaneously saint and sinner" as applied to Martin Luther?

PRAYER FOR UNITY

Read paragraph 230, then discuss:

- Together write a prayer or intercession for unity that is both global in its plea for more visible unity within the body of Christ and also contextual for your particular congregations.
- How might the Confession of St. Peter (January 18) and the Conversion of St. Paul (January 25) provide unique opportunities for Catholic and Lutheran congregations to come together for mutual prayers for unity?

EVALUATING THE PAST

Read paragraphs 231–233, then discuss:

- Reflecting upon the cultural and political contexts during the sixteenth century which contributed to the division of the Western Church, identify and discuss similar cultural and political influences which continue to foster division within the one body of Christ.

- What are some theological convictions to which your conscience is bound? How do we treat another sibling in Christ who likewise holds a conscience bound conviction that is contrary to yours? Can we find unity while holding such conflicted convictions?

CATHOLIC CONFESSION OF SINS AGAINST UNITY

Read paragraphs 234–235, then discuss:

- Catholics as well as Lutherans have spoken and acted grievously against other Christian traditions within the body of Christ. How has each of our traditions treated Eastern Orthodox members of the body of Christ? What do we have to confess together about our deeds and actions against other Christian traditions?
- How can Catholics and Lutherans collaborate to overcome anti-Semitism within our own traditions? How should Christians relate to Jews?
- Discuss your current understanding as a Catholic or a Lutheran of the papacy. Can the pope, the bishop of Rome, be a sign of unity for Lutherans? How do Catholics respond when some of their bishops take issue with statements by the pope?

LUTHERAN CONFESSION OF SINS AGAINST UNITY

Read paragraphs 236–237, then discuss:

- Lutherans: share stories about Catholics which you heard from your parents/grandparents and within your congregation that have caused you to have been prejudiced against Catholics. How has your attitude changed? What prejudices do you still hold and need to confess?
- How do Lutherans and Catholics relate to Anabaptists today? What can we learn from these historic "peace churches"?
- The Rev. Lowell G. Almen, Co-Chair of the USA Catholic-Lutheran Dialogue, outlined six key principles of dialogue:

1. A genuine, substantive dialogue must be open.
2. A dialogue must be an honest encounter. Individuals who speak must express clearly what they believe and mean. Participants in a formal dialogue must represent the position of their church as accurately and comprehensively as possible.
3. A dialogue must be fearless. Each participant must have the courage to change perceptions and perspectives.
4. A dialogue must imagine possibilities.
5. Christian charity must prevail.
6. A capacity for repentance and renewal must be possible.

How could these principles be helpful for **local** ongoing ecumenical discussions?

Lutheran-Catholic Dialogue

The Lutheran-Catholic Dialogue has been in ongoing discussions since 1965. Each "round," or set of discussions, covers a specific topic important for the life and vitality of both communions. Recent rounds have had focused discussions on "The Church as Koinonia of Salvation," "The Hope for Eternal Life," and "Ministries of Teaching: Sources, Shapes and Essential Contents" (for discerning the truth coming to us in God's Word and communicating this truth in normative teaching for today). In order to harvest the fruits of our dialogue, a Declaration on the Way (to unity) will highlight essential areas of agreement as a foundation for unity.

For information on the earlier *Joint Declaration on the Doctrine of Justification (JDDJ)*, see http://www.elca.org/en/Faith/Ecumenical-and-Inter-Religious-Relations/Bilateral#sthash.sbvdJvPs.dpuf.

DOCUMENTS PRODUCED BY THE LUTHERAN-CATHOLIC DIALOGUE IN THE UNITED STATES

The Status of the Nicene Creed as Dogma of the Church (July 7, 1965)
One Baptism for the Remission of Sins (February 13, 1966)
The Eucharist (October 1, 1967)
Eucharist and Ministry (1970)
Differing Attitudes toward Papal Primacy (1973)
Teaching Authority and Infallibility in the Church (1978)
Justification by Faith (1983)
The One Mediator, the Saints, and Mary (1990)
Scripture and Tradition (1995)
The Church as Koinonia of Salvation: Its Structures and Ministries (2004)
The Hope of Eternal Life (November 1, 2010)

ADDITIONAL INFORMATION

For additional information, please consult the ecumenical and interreligious websites of the Evangelical Lutheran Church in America and the United States Conference of Catholic Bishops' beliefs and teaching:

- http://www.elca.org/en/Faith/Ecumenical-and-Inter-Religious-Rela tions/Bilateral#sthash.sbvdJvPs.dpuf
- http://www.usccb.org/beliefs-and-teachings/ecumenical-and-interre ligious/ecumenical/lutheran/lutheran-documents.cfm

RESPONSE

Responses to the local study of *From Conflict to Communion* may be sent to:

CADEIO
c/o Ecumenical and Interreligious Affairs
3211 Fourth St. NE
Washington, D.C. 20017

LEIRN—ELCA
c/o Ecumenical and Inter-Religious
8765 West Higgins Road
Chicago, IL 60631

Common Prayer for the Ecumenical Commemoration, Lund, Sweden, October 31, 2016

Introduction

This liturgical order marks a very special moment in the journey from conflict to communion between Lutherans and Catholics. It offers an opportunity to look back in thanksgiving and confession and to look ahead, committing ourselves to common witness and continuing our journey together.

This ecumenical commemoration of the 500 years of Reformation reflects in its basic liturgical structure themes of thanksgiving, repentance, and common witness and commitment, as developed in *From Conflict to Communion*. These characteristics of common prayer mirror the reality of Christian life: shaped by God's Word, the people are sent out in common witness and service. In this particular and unique ecumenical commemoration, thanksgiving and lament, joy and repentance mark the singing and the praying as we commemorate the gifts of the Reformation and ask forgiveness for the division that we have perpetuated. Thanksgiving and lament, however, do not stand alone: they lead us to common witness and commitment to each other and for the world.

This Common Prayer was jointly prepared by the Lutheran World Federation (LWF) and the Pontifical Council for Promoting Christian Unity (PCPCU) and was used for the Joint Commemoration of the Reformation on October 31, 2016, at Lund, Sweden, when Catholics and Lutherans together launched the 500th anniversary of the Reformation.

The Joint Commemoration was presided over by His Holiness Pope Francis and Bishop Munib Younan, president of the LWF. They were assisted by the Rev. Dr. Martin Junge, the General Secretary of the LWF, and His Eminence Kurt Cardinal Koch, president of the PCPCU. The Archbishop of Uppsala, Church of Sweden, Antje Jackelén, and the Roman Catholic Bishop of Stockholm, Anders Arborelius, were the local hosts for this global event.

The Common Prayer is a template to be used and adapted for local use, among congregations or on the synodical/diocesan level.

DIRK G. LANGE,
Luther Seminary,
St. Paul, Minnesota, USA

THEO DIETER,
Institute for Ecumenical Research,
Strasbourg, France

WOLFGANG THÖNISSEN,
Johann-Adam-Möhler Institut für Ökumenik,
Paderborn, Germany

Common Prayer

From Conflict to Communion: Lutheran-Catholic
Commemoration of the Reformation

Opening

Opening Song

PRESIDER I:
In the name of the Father, and of the (+) Son, and of the Holy Spirit.
Amen.

The Lord be with you!
And also with you!

[Optional: Other opening dialogues may be used, depending on context and language.]

O Lord, open my lips
And my mouth shall proclaim your praise.

Glory to the Father, and to the Son, and to the Holy Spirit;
As it was in the beginning, is now, and will be forever. Amen.

PRESIDER I:
Dear Sisters and Brothers in Christ! Welcome to this ecumenical prayer, which commemorates the 500 years of the Reformation. For over fifty years Lutherans and Catholics have been on a journey from conflict to communion. With joy, we have come to recognize that what unites us is far greater

---

Text by the Liturgical Task Force of the Lutheran–Roman Catholic Commission on Unity than what divides us. On this journey, mutual understanding and trust have grown.

PRESIDER II:

So it is possible for us to gather today. We come with different thoughts and feelings of thanksgiving and lament, joy and repentance, joy in the gospel and sorrow for division. We gather to commemorate in remembrance, in thanksgiving and confession, and in common witness and commitment.

READER I:

In the document *From Conflict to Communion*, we read, "The church is the body of Christ. As there is only one Christ, so also he has only one body. Through baptism, human beings are made members of this body" (#219). "Since Catholics and Lutherans are bound to one another in the body of Christ as members of it, then it is true of them what Paul says in 1 Corinthians 12:26: 'If one member suffers, all suffer together; if one member is honored, all rejoice together.' What affects one member of the body also affects all the others. For this reason, when Lutheran Christians remember the events that led to the particular formation of their churches, they do not wish to do so without their Catholic fellow Christians. In remembering with each other the beginning of the Reformation, they are taking their baptism seriously" (#221).

PRESIDER I:

Let us pray!

  [Brief silence]

Jesus Christ, Lord of the church, send your Holy Spirit! Illumine our hearts and heal our memories. O Holy Spirit, help us to rejoice in the gifts that have come to the church through the Reformation, prepare us to repent for the dividing walls that we, and our forebears, have built, and equip us for common witness and service in the world.
  Amen.

Song invoking the Holy Spirit

Thanksgiving

READER I:

A reading from *From Conflict to Communion*:
"Lutherans are thankful in their hearts for what Luther and the other reformers made accessible to them: the understanding of the gospel of Jesus Christ and faith in him; the insight into the mystery of the Triune God who gives Himself to us human beings out of grace and who can be received only in full trust in the divine promise; the freedom and certainty that the gospel creates; in the love that comes from and is awakened by faith, and in the hope in life and death that faith brings with it; and in the living contact with the Holy Scripture, the catechisms, and hymns that draw faith into life" (#225), in the priesthood of all baptized believers and their calling for the common mission of the church. "Lutherans . . . realize that what they are thanking God for is not a gift that they can claim only for themselves. They want to share this gift with all other Christians" (#226).

READER II:

"Catholics and Lutherans have so much of the faith in common that they can . . . be thankful together" (#226). Encouraged by the Second Vatican Council, Catholics "gladly acknowledge and esteem the truly Christian endowments from our common heritage which are to be found among our separated brethren. It is right and salutary to recognize the riches of Christ and virtuous works in the lives of others who are bearing witness to Christ, sometimes even to the shedding of their blood. For God is always wonderful in His works and worthy of all praise" (*Unitatis Redintegratio*, chapter 1). In this spirit, Catholics and Lutherans embrace each other as sisters and brothers in the Lord. Together they rejoice in the truly Christian gifts that they both have received and rediscovered in various ways through the renewal and impulses of the Reformation. These gifts are reason for thanksgiving. "The ecumenical journey enables Lutherans and Catholics to appreciate together Martin Luther's insight into and spiritual experience of the gospel of the righteousness of God, which is also God's mercy" (#244).

PRESIDER I:

Let us pray!

[Brief silence]

Thanks be to you, O God, for the many guiding theological and spiritual insights that we have all received through the Reformation. Thanks be to you for the good transformations and reforms that were set in motion by the Reformation or by struggling with its challenges. Thanks be to you for the proclamation of the gospel that occurred during the Reformation and that since then has strengthened countless people to live lives of faith in Jesus Christ.
Amen.

Song of Thanksgiving

Repentance

READER I:
"As the commemoration in 2017 brings joy and gratitude to expression, so must it also allow room for both Lutherans and Catholics to experience the pain over failures and trespasses, guilt and sin in the persons and events that are being remembered" (#228). "In the sixteenth century, Catholics and Lutherans frequently not only misunderstood but also exaggerated and caricatured their opponents in order to make them look ridiculous. They repeatedly violated the eighth commandment, which prohibits bearing false witness against one's neighbor" (#233).

READER II:
Lutherans and Catholics often focused on what separated them from each other rather than looking for what united them. They accepted that the gospel was mixed with the political and economic interests of those in power. Their failures resulted in the deaths of hundreds of thousands of people. Families were torn apart, people imprisoned and tortured, wars fought, and religion and faith misused. Human beings suffered and the credibility of the gospel was undermined with consequences that still impact us today. We deeply regret the evil things that Catholics and Lutherans have mutually done to each other.

PRESIDER I:
Let us pray!

[Brief silence]

PRESIDER II:

O God of mercy, we lament that even good actions of reform and renewal had often unintended negative consequences.

Kyrie eleison (Lord have mercy)

PRESIDER I:

We bring before you the burdens of the guilt of the past when our forebears did not follow your will that all be one in the truth of the gospel.

Christe eleison (Christ have mercy)

PRESIDER II:

We confess our own ways of thinking and acting that perpetuate the divisions of the past. As communities and as individuals, we build many walls around us: mental, spiritual, physical, political walls that result in discrimination and violence. Forgive us, Lord.

Kyrie eleison (Lord have mercy)

Psalm 130

[The psalm can be sung on psalm tone or read by alternate whole verse.]

PRESIDERS I AND II:

[These words may be said alternately by presiders I and II.]

Christ is the way, the truth, and the life. He is our peace, who breaks down the walls that divide, who gives us, through the Holy Spirit, ever-new beginnings. In Christ, we receive forgiveness and reconciliation, and we are strengthened for a faithful and common witness in our time.

Amen

The Peace

PRESIDER II:

Let the peace of Christ rule in your hearts, since as members of one body you are called to peace.

The peace of Christ be with you always!

And also with you!

PRESIDER I:
Let us offer each other a sign of reconciliation and peace.

Sharing of peace

[During the sharing of peace, *Ubi Caritas* or another hymn may be sung.]

Gospel

READER I:
As we continue our journey from conflict to communion, let us hear the Gospel according to John:

"I am the true vine, and my Father is the vinegrower. He removes every branch in me that bears no fruit. Every branch that bears fruit he prunes to make it bear more fruit. You have already been cleansed by the word that I have spoken to you. Abide in me as I abide in you. Just as the branch cannot bear fruit by itself unless it abides in the vine, neither can you unless you abide in me. I am the vine, you are the branches. Those who abide in me and I in them bear much fruit, because apart from me you can do nothing" (John 15:1–5).

The Gospel of the Lord!
Thanks be to God!

Joint Sermon

PRESIDER I:
Together, let us confess our faith.

The Apostles' Creed

Song

Commitments: Five Imperatives

PRESIDER II:
Our ecumenical journey continues. In this worship, we commit ourselves to

grow in communion. The five imperatives found in *From Conflict to Communion* will guide us.

[A large candle is lighted after each commitment is read. The light may be taken each time from the Paschal Candle. Young people may be asked to read the five commitments, and the candles may be lit by children and families. The organ or other instrument may play the melody of a song such as "In the Lord I'll be ever thankful" (Taizé) or another song to accompany the lighting of the candles.]

1. Our first commitment: Catholics and Lutherans should always begin from the perspective of unity and not from the point of view of division in order to strengthen what is held in common even though the differences are more easily seen and experienced. (#239)

[Light a candle.]

2. Our second commitment: Lutherans and Catholics must let themselves continuously be transformed by the encounter with the other and by the mutual witness of faith. (#240)

[Light a candle.]

3. Our third commitment: Catholics and Lutherans should again commit themselves to seek visible unity, to elaborate together what this means in concrete steps, and to strive repeatedly toward this goal. (#241)

[Light a candle.]

4. Our fourth commitment: Lutherans and Catholics should jointly rediscover the power of the gospel of Jesus Christ for our time. (#242)

[Light a candle.]

5. Our fifth commitment: Catholics and Lutherans should witness together to the mercy of God in proclamation and service to the world. (#243)

[Light a candle.]

Song

Intercessory Prayer

[The person praying the intercession may be different from the previous readers.]

PRESIDER I:

"Ecumenical engagement for the unity of the church does not serve only the church but also the world so that the world may believe" (#243). Let us now pray for the world, the church, and all those in need . . .

1. God of mercy, throughout history your goodness prevails; open the hearts of all people to find you and your mercy that endures forever.
   Hear our prayer!

2. God of peace, bend that which is inflexible, the barriers that divide, the attachments that thwart reconciliation. Bring peace in this world, especially in [name countries, places . . .]. Restore wholeness among us and show us your mercy!
   Hear our prayer!

3. God of justice, healer and redeemer, heal those who suffer from illness, poverty, and exclusion. Hasten justice for those suffering under the power of evil. Give new life to all and show us your mercy!
   Hear our prayer!

4. God, rock and fortress, protect refugees, those without homes or security, all the abandoned children. Help us always to defend human dignity. Show us your mercy!
   Hear our prayer!

5. God creator, all creation groans in expectation; convert us from exploitation. Teach us to live in harmony with your creation. Show us your mercy!
   Hear our prayer!

6. God of mercy, strengthen and protect those who are persecuted for faith in you and those of other faiths who suffer persecution. Give us the courage to profess our faith. Your mercy endures forever.
   Hear our prayer!

7. God of life, heal painful memories, transform all complacency, indifference, and ignorance, pour out a spirit of reconciliation. Turn us to you and one another. Show us your mercy!
   Hear our prayer!

8. God of love, your son Jesus reveals the mystery of love among us. Strengthen that unity that you alone sustain in our diversity. Your mercy endures forever!

Hear our prayer!

9. God our sustenance, bring us together at your eucharistic table, nurture within and among us a communion rooted in your love. Your mercy endures forever!

Hear our prayer!

PRESIDER II:

In confidence that you, O God, hear our prayers for the needs of this world and for the unity of all Christians in their witness, let us pray as Jesus taught us . . .

The Lord's Prayer
Our Father . . .

PRESIDER I:

For all that God can do within us, for all that God can do without us,

Thanks be to God!

PRESIDER II:

For all in whom Christ lived before us, for all in whom Christ lives beside us,

Thanks be to God!

PRESIDER I:

For all the Spirit wants to bring us, for where the Spirit wants to send us,

Thanks be to God!

PRESIDERS (JOINTLY):

The blessing of God, Father, Son, and Holy Spirit, be with you and on your way together, now and forever.

Amen.

Song

[Other songs may be sung or a postlude played as people leave.]

Lutheran and Roman Catholic Vespers with Propers for the Unity of the Church

Compiled by the Rev. Jared R. Stahler

in collaboration with clergy and musician colleagues of three New York City parishes:

The Roman Catholic Parish of Our Saviour
Saint Stephen and Our Lady of the Scapular
and the Chapel of the Sacred Hearts of Jesus and Mary

and of

Saint Peter's Church, New York City, a Congregation of the Evangelical Lutheran Church in America

Lutheran and Roman Catholic Vespers with Propers for the Unity of the Church

A Guide for Planning Joint Parish Liturgies

The Rev. Jared R. Stahler

In commemorating the 500th anniversary of the Reformation, the Holy Spirit presents to the churches in general, and to Lutherans and Roman Catholics in particular, an ecumenical opportunity to manifest the visible unity of the church in ever-increasing fullness. While international, national, and regional events, documents, and liturgies receive much attention, the parochial context is not to be overlooked or neglected. A special fruitfulness in these local settings is the ongoing process of reception of more than fifty years of ecumenical dialogue, breakthrough, and agreement.

What follows is an outline for planning a joint Roman Catholic–Lutheran Vespers with propers for the Unity of the Church. While both ecclesial communities have continued to share—from the sixteenth century on—a common *Ordo* for this prayer office, few people today are aware of the convergence, and still fewer people from one tradition are aware of the other tradition's liturgical resources. Jointly planning and jointly praying in this way brings a tangible, local expression to the visible unity invited by the Holy Spirit and seeks to foster continued reception of ecumenical achievements.

The planning material for joint Vespers is offered in an intentionally flexible manner, following the Vespers *Ordo* and drawing on the pastoral discretion provided for in both traditions. Depending on local resources a planning team might choose to select material provided from one tradition or the other, some combination of both, or another source altogether. Planners may seek to craft one liturgy or a series of liturgies. Congregations would do well to pray Vespers together and then make use of this volume's study guide as a means of entering into conversation. Parishes may find it particularly fruitful to celebrate these Vespers on days otherwise marked by

---

Jared R. Stahler is associate pastor of St. Peter's Lutheran Church, New York City.

division: June 25, the day commemorating the presentation of the Augsburg Confession; October 31, traditionally celebrated as Reformation Day but also the day, in 1999, when the Vatican and the Lutheran World Federation signed the historic Joint Declaration on the Doctrine of Justification; or some other such day.

In all things, the goal is to draw communities into an encounter that helps each see in the other the one holy catholic and apostolic church gathered by the power of the Holy Spirit, jointly at prayer, and together proclaiming the gospel in word and deed.

Wm. B. Eerdmans Publishing Co. freely grants permission for the adaptation and reproduction of the following liturgy in bulletins and other materials produced by parishes and dioceses for use in worship services.

ABBREVIATIONS

ELW	*Evangelical Lutheran Worship*
ELW Leader	*Evangelical Lutheran Worship: Leader's Desk Edition*
W4	*Worship—Fourth Edition*

Lutheran and Roman Catholic Vespers with Propers for the Unity of the Church

Lucinarium / Service of Light
*If omitted, an opening versicle/dialogue
is followed by a proper evening hymn leading to the Psalmody.*

ELW Leader 707   W 4 #11

Hymn of light
ELW Hymn 229–231, 560–563   W 4 #13

Thanksgiving for Light
ELW Leader 708–709   W 4 #14

Psalmody
First Psalm
Psalm 141 is proper to Vespers

ELW Leader 710   W 4 #105

Psalm 110 is proper to Sunday Vespers

ELW Psalm 110   W 4 #84

*Hymns that capture the spirit of this psalm
common to both traditions include:*

ELW Hymn 835	All Creatures of Our God and King	W 4 #607
ELW Hymn 856	How Great Thou Art	W 4 #578
ELW Hymn 431	O Christ, What Can It Mean for Us	W 4 #567

Second Psalm

The Lutheran rite appoints a proper psalm for the Unity of the Church:

The Roman Catholic rite cycles in four weeks:
Week 1: Psalm 114
Psalm 113
Week 2: Psalm 115
Week 3: Psalm 111
Week 4: Psalm 112

Canticle

The Lutheran rite allows for singing of a hymn, often chosen with focus on the work of Christ, the Light of the world.	The Roman Catholic rite appoints the singing of a New Testament Canticle. Revelation 19 is proper to Sunday Vespers (W4 #131), except in Lent, when 1 Peter 2 (W4 #130) is used.

Christ- and light-centered hymns that could be sung here or elsewhere common to both traditions include:

ELW Hymn 307	Light Shone in Darkness	W4 #588
ELW Hymn 866	Siyahamba	W4 #586

Word

Both traditions have appointed cycles and allow for variation based on pastoral need. These readings highlight the visible unity of the church:

Numbers 21:4b–9	Acts 16:9–15	Saint Matthew 28:16–20
Isaiah 2:2–4	1 Corinthians 11:23–26	Saint Luke 10:25–37
Isaiah 52:7–19	Ephesians 4:1–6	Saint Luke 24:13–49
Isaiah 66:10–14	Hebrews 4:12–16	Saint John 4:5–42
Ezekiel 34:11–16	Hebrews 11:29–12:2	Saint John 17:15–23

Dialogue / Responsory

Options at ELW Leader 712	Seasonal at W4 #15

Gospel Canticle: Magnificat

ELW Leader 712	W4 #16
Other musical settings	Other musical settings
ELW Hymn 234–235, 251, 573, 723, 882	W4 #120–124

Prayers

Both traditions follow a similar pattern of prayer and have a variety of sources and formulas for intoning the text.

Jointly crafted intercessions may include a selection of these or similar petitions—one or two from each area of concern, as appropriate.

It is appropriate to begin:
Leader: In peace, let us pray to the Lord.
    Response: Lord, hear our prayer.

+ + +
The Church
For Francis and [name of local Roman Catholic bishop], and
for [name of local Lutheran bishop] and Elizabeth,
our bishops and all bishops.[1]
For [name of local Roman Catholic pastor] and [name of local Lutheran
    pastor], our pastors, and all pastors.
For all servants of the church.
For the unity of the One Holy Catholic and Apostolic Church
For common witness to the Gospel.

Each petition selected may conclude:
Leader: Let us pray to the Lord.
Response: Lord, hear our prayer.

+ + +
The government
For public servants, the government, and all who seek public office.
For those who work to bring peace, healing, and protection.
For laws that uphold equity and justice, and care of the creation.

Each petition selected may conclude:
Leader: Let us pray to the Lord.
Response: Lord, hear our prayer.

+ + +
Those in need
For those who are sick.
For those who are homeless, or without food or employment.
For those experiencing affliction or danger, especially refugees.
For those in captivity.
For those who travel.

---

1. His Holiness Pope Francis is Bishop of Rome. The Rev. Elizabeth Eaton is Presiding Bishop of the Evangelical Lutheran Church in America.

Each petition selected may conclude:
Leader: Let us pray to the Lord.
Response: Lord, hear our prayer.

+ + +
The local church
For a particular mission of the local church.
For ministries undertaken together.
For particular needs of the local church.
For those preparing for Holy Communion, baptism, etc.
For growth in common life of the two communities.

Each petition selected may conclude:
Leader: Let us pray to the Lord.
Response: Lord, hear our prayer.

+ + +
The communion of saints
In thanksgiving for local persons who have recently died.
In thanksgiving for particular saints.
In thanksgiving for Mary, Mother of Our Lord.
Commending all to Christ, Our Lord.

Each petition selected may conclude:
Leader: Let us pray to the Lord.
Response: Lord, hear our prayer.

Lord's Prayer

ELW Leader 716   W4 #18

Prayer / Collect
A prayer for the unity of the church is proper.

Christian Unity   Masses for Various Needs
ELW Leader 134   and Occasions, the Mass
                                for the Unity of Christians
                                #17 Roman Missal

Blessing and Dismissal

ELW Leader 717   W4 #19 and #20

*Hymns for the visible unity of the church or
community in Christ that could be sung here or
elsewhere common to both traditions include:*

ELW Hymn 728	Blest Are They	W4 #721
ELW Hymn 729	The Church of Christ in Every Age	W4 #785
ELW Hymn 614	There Is a Balm	W4 #646
ELW Hymn 496	One Bread, One Body	W4 #931
ELW Hymn 639	Pues si vivimos	W4 #754
ELW Hymn 819	Uyaimose	W4 #828
ELW Hymn 720	We Are Called	W4 #799
ELW Hymn 484	You Satisfy the Hungry Heart	W4 #939
ELW Hymn 424	Ye Watchers and Ye Holy Ones	W4 #886